Building a Bridge
from
"*I Can't*"
to "*I DID!*"

Creating Independent Learners Through
Culturally Responsive Teaching

Jenn Kleiber

WWW.SELFPUBLISHN30DAYS.COM

Published by Self Publish -N- 30 Days

Printed in the United States of America

ISBN: 978-1- 69676-114-7 1. Non-fiction 2. Education 3. Cultural Competence Jenn Kleiber Building a Bridge from "I Can't" to "I DID!"

Disclaimer/Warning:
This book is intended for lecture and informative purposes only. The author or publisher do not guarantee that anyone following these steps will be successful in education or teaching. The author and publisher shall have neither liability responsibility to anyone with respect to any loss or damage cause, or alleged to be caused, directly or indirectly by the information contained in this book.

Table of Contents

Acknowledgements

I would like to thank the many teachers that I have the privilege to work with and learn from—who put in the work and love and time and investment necessary to move students forward.

I'd like to thank Tonie Garza and Nora Fabela, co-founders of EL Saber Enterprises, who took a chance on me many years ago. They opened my eyes to see through a different lens, and gave me love and patience as I grew to see through it.

I would also like to thank my husband, Chris, who always supports and encourages me to stay the course, even when doubt and fear creep in, and my son, Tate, who inspires me to see through his innocent eyes and love better.

Last, but certainly not least, I thank God, who put a passion in my heart at a very young age. His grace, love and faithfulness are beyond measure.

I am very thankful to the following teachers and administrators for adding their voice, experience and expertise on this book:

Sarah Meisel
High School ELA and Sheltered
  Teacher
Colleyville Heritage High School
Colleyville, Texas

Tyra Sentell
Instructional Reading Specialist
Leadership Academy at
Maude I. Logan
Fort Worth, Texas

April Mueller
5th Grade Teacher
Messiah Lutheran School
Weldon Spring, Missouri

Jared Gibson
7th Grade Science Teacher
Watauga Middle School
Watauga, Texas

Ashley Cunningham
Sheltered Instruction Lead
Union Public School
Tulsa, Oklahoma

Amy White
8th Grade ELA Teacher
North Richland Middle School
North Richland Hills, Texas

Aristo Torres
Elementary Principal
Faith Family Academy
Dallas, Texas

**Scott Drue and
Alfonso Giardiello**
Principal and Vice Principal
Aloha-Huber Park School
Beaverton, Oregon

Introduction

I'm not an author. I'm a writer, but I'm not an author. I love to write. I write for fun every day in fact—poems, prayers, memories, reminders, blogs, lists … but I'm still not an author. So why am I writing this book? Because large groups (we like to call them "subpops" in our education jargon) are not being successful in school, and the result is horrific once they get to "real life." Our kids need help, and there are solutions, and I have to share what I've learned!

Before we jump into the meat of this book, please understand my heart. In my nearly 20 years in education, I have seen students from all backgrounds, cultures, and economic classes achieve great accomplishments and reach big dreams. I have seen resiliency and determination in students that I have had the pleasure to know. So please note, that as we talk about certain marginalized groups in this book, it does not encapsulate an entire population, because there are always those precious people that overcome the odds no matter what. I have the utmost respect for both students who are given opportunities and choose to take them and for students who create their own opportunities despite circumstances.

The issue this book addresses is the systemic problem that the education system unintentionally perpetuates. Most of us become teachers because we love students. We want to reach them in any way we can, and we are willing to go the distance to help these students overcome the odds. If you are like me, I didn't even know what the odds were for most of my students.

The lovely thing about being an educator is that although we may be in an education system that is not necessarily designed to be culturally responsive, we have the power within our own classrooms to create a system that intentionally perpetuates learning and success for *ALL* of our students! The goal of this book is to help you develop that system, first by gaining an understanding and expanding our own cultural lens, and then putting into practice strategies to reach these struggling students.

This book serves a few different purposes:

1. Become familiar with the deep cultural differences that impact learning.

2. Understand where long-term English learners, many students of color, and students of poverty are coming from: how they think, how they learn, why they have certain behaviors, and what they are searching for.

3. Understand the basics of how the brain works, and how we can make the most of the learning brain.

4. Acquire strategies and ideas for working with this unique, super talented group of students.

5. Hear testimonials from the teachers and administrators who are working in a culturally responsive environment.

The struggle is very real in schools all over the country as teachers work tirelessly to move these kids to academic success with little to no success. Teachers are trying to build the bridge for students who have shut down, struggle to build vocabulary, have minimal comprehension to take on new content, and have far greater priorities than a grade in school.

But what are the students up against? This may be the real question.

Why is it that even the most loving and patient teachers cannot seem to pull some of these students out of the academic quicksand they seemed to fall in and set them back on solid ground so that they can cross the finish line victoriously? What is pulling the students under? Why won't they help themselves?

Thank you for meeting me here. The fact that you are here at all shows that you recognize that there is a need not being met, and you are willing to help find a solution. For that, I am forever grateful. There is good and bad news—the bad news is that the journey (yes—journey. It's not an overnight fix) is long and challenging, but the good news is that these students can be reached! So let's just celebrate that for a moment, and then get to work.

> "Every child deserves a champion: an adult who will never give up on them, who understands the power of connection and insists they become the best they can possibly be."
>
> **RITA PIERSON**

PART I
The What

"The best thing about being a teacher is that it matters. The hardest thing about being a teacher is that it matters every day."

TODD WHITAKER

CHAPTER 1

The WHAT and WHY of Culture

"A culture is a way of life of a group of people—the behaviors, beliefs, values, and symbols that they accept, generally without thinking about them, and that are passed along by communication and imitation from one generation to the next."[1]

Why is culture so important? Culture affects every part of who we are and how we think and feel about life. It is the lens by which we see and understand the world. It affects how we communicate and receive messages. It only makes sense that our culture would affect the way we learn and view school. By neglecting, or by simply not knowing, the cultural perspectives of the students sitting in our classroom, we can easily miss the best ways these students learn.

I have been more and more convinced that our job as educators is not to teach; it is to *facilitate learning*. If our students aren't learning, are we really doing our jobs?

I have the privilege of spending a good part of my time leading professional development for teachers. I could stand in front of a group of people all day and train, but if the participants walked out without a single piece of knowledge, that would be on me and my ability to communicate, even if I felt I was prepared. I can blame the audience, but in the end, my message wasn't received because of the way I delivered it.

We have to be self-reflective on the learning our teaching is producing. Our goal is to create independent learners, learners who have the cognitive capacity to problem solve and think at higher levels. If we are not creating independent learners with certain groups of students, perhaps the issue is not the teaching or the learning. Perhaps it's the cultural perspective we are missing.

What Culture Defines

In *Why Culture Counts*, by Tileston and Darling (2008), we see that culture trumps basically everything else in determining how the students will learn and what knowledge, experience and skills they will bring to the classroom. A child's culture defines:

- What they will focus their attention on
- How they interpret the world and give it meaning
- What background knowledge they bring to learning
- How they will value that learning[2]

Let's take a deeper look at each of these points.

WHAT THEY WILL FOCUS THEIR ATTENTION ON

How often do we stand at the front of the classroom and pretty much beg for the attention of the students? I remember pleading, "Come on guys! Stay with me! We just have to get through a few more slides!" If we have to continue to ask, clearly our content or task is not engaging enough to hold their attention. So, what does this mean?

We have to teach them how to solve two-step problems with variables in them. Right? Right! But this is where the learning styles, differentiation and scaffolding come into play, which we will discuss more in Chapter 7. We have to understand that different cultures emphasize and place value on different topics, social situations, and learning modalities. By understanding these cultural perspectives and using them as a strength, any content can be taught and learned more effectively.

For example, students from a Latino background often emphasize family, relationships, and hard work. So, in the example of solving two-step problems with variables in a 7th grade math class, having students listen and copy the teacher step-by-step for an entire class period may not be the most effective approach. Having students work together, to rely on each other for understanding, to check to see if they got it correct, and lean on each other to problem-solve will engage these students more in the learning.

HOW THEY INTERPRET THE WORLD AND GIVE IT MEANING

We will discuss cultural bias a little later in the chapter, but every person brings their own cultural lens to the table, including our students. If you and your students come from different cultural backgrounds, understanding from the beginning that you probably look at day-to-day events in the world differently will greatly help your understanding and bridging.

Take a look at the chart of Common Cultural Ideas. While these do not encapsulate every family within these demographics, it can give us an idea of the family structures of many of our students.

Common Cultural Ideas			
Caucasian	**African American**	**Latino**	**Asian**
The mother is often equal to the father. She can work outside of the home, and often makes decisions for the family.	The mother tends to be the authority in the home. This authoritative role can also be held by the grandmother or even older siblings.	The mother serves the family. The father typically brings in income and makes decisions for the family. The mother takes care of domestic issues.	The mother serves the family. The father typically brings in income and makes decisions for the family. The mother takes care of domestic issues.
The family is typically nuclear, with the parents and children living in the same household.	The family is often extended, with grandparents, aunts, uncles and cousins living in the same household.	The family is often extended, with grandparents, aunts, uncles and cousins living in the same household.	The family is often extended, with grandparents, aunts, uncles and cousins living in the same household.
Women are equal. Authority is not based on gender.	Women are the authority inside and outside of the home.[2]	Women hold very little authority outside of the home.[3]	Women hold very little authority outside of the home.[4,5]

Why does this matter in the classroom? Well, let's think about it.

I once had a class that I became very close with and was able to have some candid conversations with students by the end of the year. At the time, I was a 30-year-old Caucasian teacher, just as a point of reference. At the end of the school year, I asked them to be honest about their "first impressions" of me and the class when they walked into the classroom. Here's what they said:

Mary (Caucasian): "I had no thought other than you looked young and nice."

Keisha (African American): "Oh I thought you were going to be a pushover, but then I liked you because you were fair, so it was all good."

Jose (Latino): "Another white teacher. Another class that won't matter—you know I already had my job."

Phu (Vietnamese): "I didn't really think anything about you. I just wanted to know how hard the class was going to be."

These thoughts made sense when you look at the deep belief systems of each ethnicity:

Caucasian: Cultural lens typically respects authority for being authority—the expectation is that there will probably be a Caucasian teacher.

African American: Cultural lens may hold the belief that Caucasian women are not as strong as African American women, and that there is an element of unfairness from the teacher to the students.

Latino: Cultural lens may not see school as a necessarily relevant piece to the puzzle of a life that is already put into motion; therefore, the teacher is not necessarily a relevant piece.

Asian: Education tends to be very important in this culture, regardless of the teacher.

This was so enlightening to me, and I wish I would have known it at the beginning of the year, instead of at the end. All four of these students needed to be approached differently by me. Honestly, at that point, I realized that I had missed some valuable instructional time because I hadn't approached some of them the right way from the beginning.

WHAT BACKGROUND KNOWLEDGE THEY BRING TO LEARNING

This is *so important*! Background knowledge primarily encompasses three different components:

1. Previous knowledge

2. Prior experience

3. Vocabulary

If you have worked with English learners at all, you have heard about background knowledge!

Previous Knowledge

I'll never forget a time when this concept became so blaringly apparent to me. I was teaching English I to a group of English learners, none of whom had been in the country more than three years. The high school I taught at had school-wide book reads, and this particular year, they had chosen *The Book Thief*, by Markus Zusak. This book is written from the perspective of the character named Death, takes place during the Holocaust, and follows a German family who is harboring a Jewish man in their basement, while the brother is fighting for the Nazis.[6]

So, I decide that my class is also going to read this 300+ page book (I was ambitious back then). I decide to take about 15 minutes to build a little background before we start this book. I ask, "What can you tell me about the Holocaust?" Nothing. "What about Nazis?" Crickets. "Germany? The Jewish people?" Still … nothing. Then one precious girl raises her hand and says, "Oh, like Anne Frank? My sister is reading that book." And that was it. That was the extent of the knowledge of the 25 15-year olds sitting in my class. Needless to say, *The Book Thief*, in all its abstract language and parallel plot structures, was not the best way to introduce this concept.

Learning new concepts connects and builds onto what we already know, even at a very young age. A four-year-old learning to count already knows concepts like "more" and "less." A kindergartener learning to add can count. All learning connects to previous learning. If we don't know what the student already knows (or doesn't

know), how can we connect the learning for them? And if we wait for the students to make their own connections, we could be wasting valuable instructional time. We have to be intentional as teachers to connect new learning to prior knowledge.

Here's another thing to consider: dependent learners, learners who can't seem to do complex tasks without continuous support, struggle to recall information from their long-term memory. This isn't saying that the knowledge isn't in their long-term memory, but they just struggle to recall it on their own. Because this can look like the students have no knowledge of a particular concept, we can feel like we need to completely reteach, or like the gaps are too big to learn grade-level strategies. Actually, an intentional strategy can bridge the learning quickly, and open these students up to new learning.

Prior Experiences

Equally as important as previous knowledge are organic, authentic experiences that the students are bringing to the table. I'll never forget another time I was working with a newcomer from Iraq. He had been in the country for just a few months, and his English II class was doing research on social issues. He had the rubric in front of him for completing a research paper, but with very little English, reading the articles, navigating the research, and writing the paper was proving more than difficult. He was able to explain to me that he was writing his paper on war. We tried looking a few ideas up, and then he looked at me, and in broken English said, "Can I just write my story? I've lived in war my whole life." Wow. Yes. When he was able to write from a familiar place, we could work more on

the organization and sentence structure needed, and a lot of learning took place that day, for him and me.

Students from different ethnic and socio-economic cultures bring experiences to the classroom that, quite honestly, my own child will probably never have. As teachers, when we can capitalize on these, we increase learning and engagement tenfold.

On the flip side, there also may be many experiences that we think are common, everyday experiences that many of our students will never have had the opportunity to see or do. I remember teaching a group of ninth graders in a high poverty, urban area in Central Texas. We were about to read a nonfiction text on tsunamis, and I wanted to give them an idea of what a tsunami was, so I showed them some videos.

I could tell they still weren't getting it when I was describing "waves as tall as a 10-story building!" Then it dawned on me that not only did none of them have a concept of a tsunami (which I expected), they also didn't have a concept of a 10-story building! A quick trip to the window showed them that we were on the second story. I had them look up to the sky to imagine eight more floors. This at least brought out some "oohs" and "aahs" that made me think they started to grasp the concept of waves that high. It didn't take long to make that connection, but it had to be intentional, and I almost missed the opportunity altogether.

Vocabulary

Vocabulary! Vocabulary! Vocabulary! I cannot emphasize this point enough! This is so important that I have designated an entire section to it later in the book. Intentional, explicit vocabulary instruction is

non-negotiable with students of poverty and English learners. One of the biggest causes of the ever-increasing academic gap is the lack of vocabulary, and the difficulty in acquiring new academic language. We cannot overlook this as we jump into new texts and concepts.

HOW THEY WILL VALUE THAT LEARNING

Students looking through a different cultural lens may value learning differently. Some will value grades, while others will value graduation. Some will value the challenge, and some will value the cooperative learning. Some will value the problem solving. If grades are the primary leverage teachers are providing for the measurement of "learning," we are leaving *many* students behind.

Surface Culture Verses Deep Culture

Before we continue any further, it's important to understand that there are different levels of culture. We are going to discuss two levels: surface and deep. Surface culture refers to the customs, traditions, clothes, food, and other parts of the culture that are usually visual to others. This is a very beautiful piece to learn about your students and can help you connect with them on so many levels. It is important to note the difference between surface culture and deep culture.

Deep culture refers to the deep seeded thoughts, feelings and beliefs that a majority of the people in one cultural group share. I have found that at times, we may not even realize that there is a thought, mindset or belief system in our deep culture that is different from other cultures. We often just believe that our deep culture is the

way it is or should be, and when others behave in a way that doesn't fit with our deep culture, it can cause offense or can make us upset.

Let me give you an example of this. One of my very best friends is an African American woman named Tyra. This precious woman is one of my all-time favorite people with which to spend time. However, I quickly noticed that no matter what we were doing, if one of her sisters or her mother called, she stopped whatever we were doing and answered the phone and proceeded to have a lengthy conversation (usually on speaker phone) about whatever they needed to visit about. At first, this was somewhat frustrating to me, because my phone was put away. If I received a call, I either texted back that I would call back later or just let it go to voicemail. However, as we are going to see in the next section, Tyra's deep culture is collectivist, and she values the relationship with her family over any other activity or person. When her family calls, she answers. No questions asked. I eventually just joined in the conversations with her sisters and mother, and we are all friends to this day. However, I had to move from frustration to understanding, because to Tyra, she didn't realize that there was even a difference in our deep cultural beliefs. If my family called, she would fully expect me to answer the phone as well.

Our Own Cultural Lens — Collectivist and Individualist

"It is what it is." Traffic, other peoples' actions, the weather, the way dinner comes out of the oven sometimes. Using this phrase is appropriate to many situations we encounter in life to help us accept the

things we cannot change. We also cannot control how our cultural lens was *formed*. Our lens comes from our community, environment, family, religion, and even country, state and area we were born and raised. However, we can adjust and adapt the lens we choose to look through moving forward. We only know what we know, so the more we know, the more we see. The more we know and understand our own cultural lens, the more we will understand the way other people perceive the world. The more we understand differences, the less frustrating and scary they can be.

Another concept that is crucial in understanding how culture links to learning is having a deep understanding of the differences between the collectivist and individualistic cultures. These are two very different lenses in which to look at the world. This is a topic that is very near and dear to my heart, because I looked at this totally wrong for a lot of years in my classroom. I can think back to the things I did and said (with good intentions, mind you), and shake my head at how misguided and naïve I was.

The **collectivist culture** tends to emphasize the needs and goals of the group as a whole over the needs and desires of the individual. Relationships are key, and often take priority over individual accomplishments. A person's identity is often found within the community they live and work. Cultures originating in Asia, Central America, South America and Africa tend to lean toward a collectivist culture.[7]

The **individualistic culture** emphasizes the individual over the group. Common goals of the individualist culture are autonomy and independence. Individual rights are important in this culture, and often times there is emphasis on being unique or standing out. Dependence on other people can be looked down upon and even

considered shameful. Cultures in North America and Western Europe tend to be individualistic.[8]

Why are these differences important? Many professions, such as international business, psychology, and the medical fields are already studying these differences in order to promote success in their varying fields, but how does this translate to your students in your classroom? Let's think about this!

For a group of students who come from a collectivist background, what are they typically going to value? They will value:

- Relationships with the teacher

- Relationships within the classroom unit/small group

- Relationships with friends

- Cooperative learning to problem solve

- Harmony within the group

- The good of the family over the individual education

Let's talk through a few scenarios that may play out with students from a collectivist culture.

Scenario 1: Friend Crying in the Bathroom

One of your middle school girls comes running into class seven minutes after the bell has rung. When you come to a stopping point in your directions, you walk over to her desk, bend down quietly, and ask why she was late. She tells you that her best friend is having a family issue at home and was crying in the bathroom. *How do you handle this, knowing you are dealing with a student from a collectivist background?*

Scenario 1:
Friend crying in the bathroom

Collectivist Response

"I love that you are such a good friend. You know that I need you here at the start of class though because a) I don't know where you are and I already counted you absent, b) it's a rule that you're here on time, and c) we get started with learning right away. So next time, just come let me know what's going on, and I'll either write you a pass, or maybe even get the counselor to go check on her."

Individualistic Response

"You know the rules. You have to take care of yourself and get to class on time. You can talk to your friends during lunch. You're tardy if you're not here on time. One more time and you have detention. You've got to get here!"

Scenario 2: Is This for a Grade?

Every time you pass out a student task, at least four students raise their hands and ask, "Hey Miss! Is this for a grade?" This makes you think that a grade is their only leverage, as if it's not for a grade, they won't do it. But what you realize is that many of your students aren't turning it in anyway. If they are turning it in, it's not their best work, and they are just doing enough to get by. *How do you handle this, knowing you are dealing with a student from a collectivist background?*

Scenario 2
Is this for a grade?

Collectivist Response

"I haven't decided what I'm taking a grade on yet, but what I'm listening for is that everyone in the group is reading their section, identifying the conflicts in the story, and then determining how the dialogue between the characters is leading to the conflicts. I'm also listening for every person's opinion on how the dialogue could change to have a different outcome on the conflict. The chart is a guide for you to document your conversation and your thoughts."

Individualistic Response

"Yes, you will turn the chart in at the end of class. Everyone will need to turn in their own chart on dialogue and conflict. You can work together on it, but everyone will get their own grade."

Scenario 3: Work Versus School

You have a student who seems to have very little motivation in school. He tries to put his head down in your class, and you struggle to engage him in the content or the tasks. After getting to know him, you realize that every day after school, and every weekend, he is working with his dad's roofing company. He makes a decent wage and is helping his family out financially. He's also trying to buy himself a car. He has already told you that he will work this business after he graduates, and eventually it will be his. His two brothers and his uncles also work this business. *How do you handle this, knowing you are dealing with a student from a collectivist background?*

Scenario 3:
Work verses school

Collectivist Response

"You work so hard! I really admire and respect you for your work ethic and your drive to have this company. Let's really talk about how what we are learning is relevant to what you're doing for work, and we can talk about the homework load if you can bring me examples from your work."

Individualistic Response

"I know you have a job, but you've got to get this work done here. If you can just stay focused in class, you can get it done and not have to worry about it after school. You need the grades to pass!"

Scenario 4: Sick Grandmother

You notice one of your students seems pretty distracted in class. She is typically a good student, but seems to be shutting down. When you have a one-on-one conversation with her, she tells you that her grandmother is very sick in Mexico, and her family is planning to leave that weekend. She doesn't know how long they will be gone, but assumes they will stay until the grandmother is either well or passes away. She knows this will make it hard for her to complete her school work, but she wants to visit her grandmother, and that takes precedence over her education. *How do you handle this, knowing you are dealing with a student from a collectivist background?*

Scenario 4: Sick grandmother

Collectivist Response

"I'm so sorry about your grandmother. I know that is so hard. Let's get you some work together so that you can try to stay up in school, and if you can be on the internet, I'll have things posted in our class social media group, and we can communicate that way. I want you to keep me updated on your grandmother."

Individualistic Response

"I'm so sorry about your grandmother. I know that is so hard. Unfortunately, you can't miss that much school and keep your grades up. I'll get some worksheets together for you, but I don't see how you're going to keep up. We can't just stop our lives when a family member gets sick. You really need to consider staying here."

Scenario 5: Multiple Families in One Household

You are on duty outside of the school building one morning when you see your student get out of his mother's car, along with five other students, four of whom you don't recognize. After speaking with the student, you realize that the mother's sister has gone back to jail, and your student's mother has taken in her four students, along with the three that she already has. Doing the math, you realize that's one adult and seven children in a two-bedroom apartment. *How do you handle this, knowing you are dealing with a student from a collectivist background?*

Scenario 5:
Multiple families in one household

Collectivist Response

"Wow! What a great mom and family member to help out the rest of the family. How do you feel about your living arrangement? Is it difficult? Do you spend a lot of time caring for the other children? I know it's difficult to study at home. Would you like to eat lunch in here so you can have a quiet place to work and study?"

Individualistic Response

"I know you have a lot of kids living in your home right now, and you're obviously not getting a good night's rest because you're tired. You're going to need to figure out how to get your work done, or stay for tutorials."

Scenario 6: Fight for a Friend

You hear a commotion in the hallway, and you run out to find one of your favorite students (I know we as teachers don't actually say we have favorites, but we all do!) in a fight with another student. When you are able to get the students separated enough to talk to your student, you find out that the previous afternoon, after school, the other student had hit one of his best friends. *How do you handle this, knowing you are dealing with a student from a collectivist background?*

Scenario 6:
Fight for a friend

Collectivist Response

"I understand fighting for a friend, and I love the loyalty and protective spirit you have, but there's a no tolerance policy at school, and you have to understand the consequences of fighting at school. Let's talk through some other ways to show loyalty and protection for your friend—and maybe it's just that you handle this off campus."

Individualistic Response

"There's never a reason to fight, and there's NEVER a time to fight at school. Now you're going to be the one in trouble—it doesn't matter the reason why. You have to think about consequences!"

"Typical" school philosophies that may not jive with the collectivist society:

- The goal is to get the best grade possible
- Give individual grades for group work
- Tutorials and/or homework are more important than outside work
- Sickness is the only reason to miss school
- Being on time to class is a priority
- College is a must for a "good job"
- Have individual "playlists" or "work at your own pace" systems

Now I want you to take a moment and think about your own cultural perspective. Where do you fall on this spectrum? I'm sure most of us have some outlier characteristics of both cultures (for example, I'll take in any family member or friend who needs a place to stay—just as my husband!), but I'm all about being a problem-solver and taking care of myself, and not always the best at asking for help.

If you came from a middle class, Caucasian family, you probably fall more in the individualistic category. If you are African American, Asian, Middle Eastern or Latino, you probably see more of yourself in the collectivist cultures. *How are you looking at your school, district or classroom? Are you expecting an individualist response from a collectivist student? Could you shift your instruction and classroom setup to reach the students from both cultures?*

Depending on how you respond to these scenarios will determine if you set up a culturally responsive classroom with high expectations

and a focus on learning, or whether you will draw the line and set up a teacher versus student mentality. Setting up a teacher versus student mentality is one of the best ways to kill the learning climate in a classroom. Students from a collectivist background put relationships ahead of everything else. It's not always easy to work your way into a relationship with students from a collectivist culture, because they have such a tight-knit network. If you don't put the work in to build this relationship, you cannot expect to push them towards learning. And if you tear down the relationship by devaluing their core values within their culture, you can't expect them to allow you into their inner circle.

As we go deeper into culturally responsive teaching in this book, we will continue to dive into what we, as the educators, can do in the classroom to facilitate the highest achievement possible for all students.

Chapter 1 At a Glance

- We all have a cultural lens with which we see the world.
- Understanding our students' cultural lenses will help us reach them in the classroom.
- It's important to understand the difference between the collectivist and the individualist culture.
- Determining the background your students bring, and building the background before teaching a new concept, can put everyone on the same playing field in learning.

Let's Process

1. Do you come from an individualist or collectivist culture?

2. Think about the students in your classroom or on your campus. Do they come from a collectivist or individualist culture?

3. How do you validate the deep culture of your students?

Strategies for Implementation

If you want to determine your own cultural lens, visit the *Cultural Lens Survey* in the Appendix. Also, if you would like to give your students a survey, feel free to copy the *Cultural Survey for Students*. This is a great way to learn more about your students.

Favorite Resources on This Topic:

Why Culture Counts, Darling and Tilston[2]

Culturally Responsive Teaching and the Brain, Zaretta Hammond[9]

Academic Vocabulary for English Learners, EL Saber Enterprises[10]

CHAPTER 2

Learn or Protect: The Survival Mode Struggle

"Our children are only as brilliant as we allow them to be."
— Eric Micha'el Leventhal

*W*hat type of teacher does it take to effectively facilitate culturally responsive teaching? If you think about the differentiation that needs to occur, the high level of expectations that must be set, and the willingness to learn and grow as demographics change, the *best* teachers need to be the teachers in a culturally responsive classroom. It needs to be teachers who have had professional development on this topic, and have specific strategies, and a *willingness* (notice the pattern?) to implement new strategies and try new ideas! A teacher in a culturally responsive classroom *must* believe that all students can learn at high levels, and set high expectations with the supports and scaffolds in place to let the students know that they can and will be successful.

Being a forward thinking teacher, willing to do whatever it takes for our students, often starts with being self-reflective. It also starts with an awareness of the world and a willingness to have the difficult conversations with others and ourselves.

We cannot overlook the achievement gaps between white children and children of color any more.[1] Data has shown us that historically, and currently, our system is not meeting the needs of these groups of students. Research continues to reveal that Latino and African American students are still scoring a few grade levels behind their white counterparts.[2] This is unacceptable, and a solvable issue, but we have to determine what's causing this problem first.

Let's take a moment to differentiate between dependent and independent learners. When students are denied the productive struggle that is required for deep learning to take place, they become dependent on the assistance, and more importantly, on the teacher who provides the assistance. When students haven't been given the opportunity to build the cognitive capacity to problem-solve and fight through the productive struggle, they lack self-efficacy and autonomy, and they don't become independent learners. We often do this unintentionally and with pure motives, but when we "dumb down" curriculum or expectations, or spoon-feed answers, we are indeed hurting our students.

Zaretta Hammond (2015) states that, "Classroom studies document the fact that underserved English learners, poor students, and students of color routinely receive less instruction in higher order skills development than other students."[3] Because this population of students often enters school with gaps in their vocabulary, as educators, we feel like we are constantly trying to play "catch-up."

We can get so stuck on trying to set the foundational skills that we forget about building the cognitive skills needed to think at higher

levels. This is the beginning of creating dependent learners. Zaretta Hammond communicates this systemic problem so well when she states the following:

> "As educators, we have to recognize that we help maintain the achievement gap when we don't teach advance cognitive skills to students we label as "disadvantaged" because of their language, gender, race, or socio-economic status. Many children start school with the small learning gaps, but as they progress through school, the gap between African American and Latino and White students grows because we don't teach them how to be independent learners."[3]

We will spend the better part of this book looking at how to create independent learners.

When we label students, we have a tendency to do the following:

- Underestimate what disadvantaged students are intellectually capable of doing

- Postpone more challenging and interesting work until we believe they have mastered the "basics"

- Focus on "low-level basics" and deprive students of meaningful context for learning and practicing higher-order thinking processes[3]

With that in mind, and with a determination to create independent learners, I think it's helpful to understand how and why learning takes place.

The brain is a very powerful tool, and we can take comfort in the fact that the brain, quite often, operates apart from the apparent will of the human being.

There are two truths that are crucial for understanding how the brain learns new information.

Two truths about the brain:

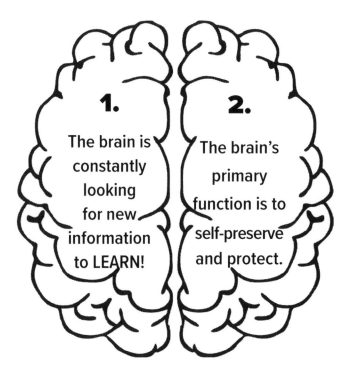

1.
The brain is constantly looking for new information to LEARN!

2.
The brain's primary function is to self-preserve and protect.

First, the brain is constantly looking for new information. The plasticity in the brain is constantly growing and forming. It is curious, and is looking for new things to observe, sounds to hear, and things to learn. So take heart—the brain WANTS to learn! We can know that our students are always subconsciously seeking to learn. They

may not be learning the content *you* want them to learn, but their brain is seeking!

But there is a catch …

The brain's primary function is to self-preserve. It is our main defense mechanism. This protect and preserve function of the brain trumps all other functions.

So what do these two truths tell us? There are so many intricate functions of the brain, and I highly recommend Eric Jenson's, *The Learning Brain,* (1995), for a more in-depth look at its capabilities. But here are the three parts of the brain I want us to think about:

1. The recticular activating system

2. The amygdala

3. The hippocampus

The Protector's Brain

The Recticular Activating System (RAS) scans the environment 24/7 for signs of threats. These are not just physical threats. This is any threat to comfort, well-being or physical health. When the RAS senses a threat, it immediately sends a signal to the amygdala. This happens subconsciously, meaning the person (or student) cannot help or control when this happens.

The amygdala triggers at least one of four responses: fight, flight, freeze or appease.

RAS (Recticular Activating System)
• Scans the environment 24/7 for threats
• Sends reports to amygdala

Amygdala
Fight, flight, freeze or appease

Let's take a look at what this means for students in a classroom.

A student feels threatened by either the teacher's response, a peer's comment, or a self-imposed thought ("I'm not a good reader; I can't be called on to read out loud!"). If a student's response is to fight, that could look like a rude comment back to the teacher or an outburst to another student. If their response is flight, this could look like a quick hand raised to go to the bathroom or nurse, or a head down with the hood up. The student basically retreats out of the situation. If their response is to freeze, they literally stop in their tracks. We get the blank look, the shrug of the shoulders, or the refusal to answer— probably because they can't come up with a thought at that time.

And last, but not least, if the student's response is to appease (this is often my own kid), you may get the quick, "yes, ma'am," so that you will stop talking to them, but their brains are not open to learning. We still have to recognize this as a response to threat, and lower the affective filter enough to bring the students back to a place where their brains can take in new information, process content, and make decisions.

That leads us into the next area to discuss: the affective filter.

The Affective Filter

Have you ever quietly redirected a student, and he shoots back with a totally inappropriate anger response?

Does it seem like it takes your students *an eternity* to get their resources and supplies and get started on a task?

Do you see your students disengage halfway through class?

Have you ever talked to a student about missing work in another teacher's class, and hear the response, "She doesn't like me. I'm not talking to her."

What causes these responses?

Stephen Krashen proposed the Affective Filter Hypothesis in 1982, and while it hasn't gone without criticism, it is a great concept to keep in mind. The hypothesis states that factors such as stress, boredom, failure, and dislike of a person or content cause the affective filter to rise, therefore lowering language acquisition and learning. When the student feels motivated, comfortable and successful, the affective filter lowers, opening the door for language acquisition and learning. See the chart on the next page[4]:

AFFECTIVE FILTER HYPOTHESIS

High Affective Filter	Low Affect Filter
Students experience stress.	Students become risk-takers as they manipulate language.
Students feel anxious and self-conscious.	Students feel safe in making mistakes without judgement and constant correction.
The lack of self-confidence might inhibit success in acquiring the second language.	Students feel empowered to interact with their peers and seek out models of language.
Students are reluctant to participate and seek out opportunities to collaborate.	Students feel safe in answering questions and sharing their thinking with peers and the teacher.
If modifications are not being made, the students will experience boredom and disinterest.	

As you can see, when the affective filter is low, the environment is conducive for higher level thinking and real learning. If what we are doing in our class **raises the affective filter** of students, we need to figure out how to lower it!

There are many practical ways to lower the affective filter, but I want to start with creating a positive environment.

Obviously, we all want and strive for our classrooms to be a positive environment, but is it? Here are some thoughts:

CREATE A POSITIVE ENVIRONMENT

- *Greet students with a smile, handshake or high five, and a positive comment as they walk in the room.* Many of their

affective filters are up due to a previous class, or an event that even happened before they got to school or in the hallway. Creating a positive vibe, and letting them know that you are glad they are in your class, goes a long way for lowering the affective filter.

- *Make a positive contact home.* For many struggling students, behavior problems are par for the course (which makes total sense now that we know about the amygdala). With these students, the only phone calls home they get are for teachers to elicit the help of the parent in correcting behavior. While I'm not opposed to this (in fact, I encourage it), if there hasn't been positive contact already made, this can send a message, primarily, "I can't handle your student and I need help"—which can be translated to "I don't like your kid."

  This message gets received loud and clear by the parents and the student. I use my own child as an example of this. I received an email the other day that simply said, "Can you please talk to Tate about talking during tests? I had to correct him twice." Now, what message does this send to me? "Your kid is driving me crazy and can't get it together." *Except,* I know that his teacher LOVES him, and has told me many times how awesome he thinks my kid is. Because he has so many positive interactions with me about Tate, when I received this email, the message I received was, "Let's work together on this," and there were absolutely no negative thoughts that went through my mind about my son's teacher. I was also completely willing to talk to my kid. This was not the case with a teacher he had a few years ago when he was in kindergarten. He got in trouble almost every day moving to carpet time. I got to the point where I was almost rolling my eyes I was so tired hearing about how Tate came to carpet time with too much energy.

Let's talk for a moment about parents from the collectivist culture. We've already discussed how this culture is, above all else, relational. If we want to build a partnership with these families, we must put in the work to build the relationship before calling them to action (come to a parent-teacher night, talk to their child about behavior, etc.).

- *If your student is not in your classroom, check on them.* Are they home sick? Make a quick phone call. Are they in In-School Suspension (or a variation of this punishment)? Go, check on them. You are lowering their affective filter for when they do return to your class.

- *Praise and affirm often.* An important piece to lowering the affective filter is the student's comfort level with asking and answering questions. Praising the learning and effort, as opposed to just "right" and "wrong," creates the positive climate needed for students to take the risk that processing, learning and building language (which we are going to talk about in the next chapter) requires.

Here are some suggestions.

- Checkmarks on their work for staying focused and staying on task

- Specific praise for thinking—"I love the thought process you are using." "I really like the way you used problem-solving skills there." "Great job debating that topic respectfully. I appreciate you both sharing your thoughts on that."

- Feedback on journal prompts

- Specific praise on grades—"You brought this grade up 20 points! I like the way you used your strategies! That really helped."

PROVIDE APPROPRIATE SUPPORTS AND SCAFFOLDS

One of the keys to moving students into being independent learners is to build their self-efficacy. This is the belief that they have the resources to complete a task or solve a problem on their own. We know that many of the students in the sub-population we are focusing on need a little extra support to fill in the gaps. But it does *not* mean that with these supports, they can't do it on their own. We have to pull ourselves out of the equation sometimes:

- *Build anchor charts with the students.* When teaching a new concept, building an anchor chart with the students helps them connect with new concepts. The anchor chart then stays up and visible in the classroom as a reference point for the student. Then, if they get stuck on the application piece, instead of you jumping in to "save them," you refer them to the anchor chart.

- *Teach students to take and use meaningful notes.* Having students who are behind in literacy, or not proficient in language, copy notes off of a slide show <u>does not</u> create meaning or learning. Most likely, they are copying one letter at a time, which brings no comprehension and takes *forever*. It can also raise the affective filter because it is not a meaningful task and can create boredom.

- *Provide linguistic accommodations.* It is important to understand that Long-Term English learners and students of poverty may speak fluently in social language, but their academic language, and the ability to acquire new academic language, plays a key role in their struggle. Providing linguistic accommodations, such as sentence frames for writing and speaking, visuals for vocabulary, and chunking information in text and instruction, can be very effective in lowering the affective filter.

- *Know the students' levels.* If you are working with English learners, and even Long-Term ELs, it is important to know their proficiency levels. This helps you set linguistic goals with the students, know the specific linguistic skills to build and accommodate appropriately.

PROVIDE RELEVANT TASKS

As we discussed in the first chapter, most of these students are not motivated by grades alone. They need to know that what they are doing is for a reason and contributes to a bigger picture:

- *Avoid busy work.* Students know the difference between a task that leads to learning and a task that is given to fill time or allow the teacher to catch up on grades. We've all done it, but don't expect a good output if the task isn't relevant.

- *Set a learning target for the task.* Be transparent in the learning. "After you complete this task, you will have learned _____." This automatically sets a purpose for their task. As the teacher, this will help you plan more relevant and aligned tasks as well. Ask yourself, *"Does this task get the students to the learning they need or does it just keep them busy?"*

- *Move the goal from task-oriented to learning-oriented.* Instead of "Complete the flow map of the important events in the story," move to "Discover how the characters' actions impact the conflict by writing in the key events that occur in the story."

PROVIDE CLEAR DIRECTIONS

Do the students know what to do? Such a basic question, but we've all been there. You give directions for a project or task the students are to do, say "Get started!" and the majority just look at you with blank looks, until the one kid raises his hand and says, "Miss, what are we supposed to do?" (Insert eye roll here.) We can immediately blame the students for not listening, or we can adjust our methods:

- *Post directions*—all directions. Believe it or not, students want to know what to do. We don't go to the store, buy a desk, and then listen to the sales person give us directions on how to put it together. There are directions in the box. We have to follow them. Our students have so much in

their minds, in addition to the normal directions in the classroom. Give them the directions in writing and refer them back to them when they have questions. This is also a step towards autonomy.

- *Give roles.* Does each student know what they should be doing? Don't leave it up to the students to determine roles in a group (unless you have already taught them and practiced often). If you want students to discuss in partners, tell them which student is going to start the conversation. For example, "Partner A has the longest hair. Partner A will answer the question. Partner B will respond with *Agree* or *Disagree* and then give an additional thought."

PROVIDE ORDER

- *Have a specific process and procedure for the transition times in your class, such as entering the classroom, moving from task to task, leaving the classroom, etc.* When students walk into a classroom, or start a new task, and don't know exactly what to do, the affective filter immediately begins to rise. Having a system for transition times immediately provides a comfort of the *known* that students need. It also establishes the understanding that it is time to be ready to learn.

- *Have clear guidelines for turning in homework and classwork.* We know that many LTELs and students of poverty struggle to turn in work. Having clear guidelines for this expectation is helpful in building this habit of turning in work.

- *Have a clear expectation of what students should do if they need help.* Do they raise their hand? Do they ask a peer? (Be very careful with this—are they comfortable asking peers? Do the peers have the answer? Do they know how to help?) Do they change a color of cups to show the teachers they need help? Do they look at their notes or anchor charts? Make this clear! Many of these students have not built up the grit they need to problem-solve, so you will need to help them with the strategies for moving forward.

Let's look at a few scenarios where the affective filter may come into play. How would you handle these situations as a culturally responsive teacher intentionally trying to lower the affective filter?

Scenario 1

It is the beginning of a new unit, and you, as the teacher, need to introduce several new vocabulary words and concepts. Currently, you have planned for the students to look up 10 words, write the definitions down, and write them in a sentence. Then you have a 12 slide PowerPoint prepared to introduce the concepts, in which the students will take notes from the slides.

Scenario 2

The morning class has just started. You have the directions posted on the board, but you notice Juan is sitting at his desk with his head down. You walk over and say, "Good morning, Juan, do you need a pencil to get started?" Juan responds, "Why are you always messing with me?!"

> ### Scenario 3
>
> The students are about to enter your classroom, but a teacher is talking to you at the door. You still need to run to your box in the teachers' lounge, and you don't know exactly what you are going to do in the classroom.

In Scenario 1, students are not going to find relevance in these tasks. While they will probably start off being compliant, boredom will kick in, and you will find yourself redirecting. "Get back on task." "Keep up with us." "Write quicker." "Stop talking." Instead, perhaps you could give students the new words, show pictures or visuals of each word to pre-teach, and then teach the words as you come to them in context. With the new concepts, teach students to take meaningful notes, but then give processing time every few concepts to allow students to process and discuss the new vocabulary and information.

In Scenario 2, the teacher can decide to take the outburst personally, or he or she can view the situation from the understanding that the student is responding in "fight" mode. If the teacher engages the student in the "fight," the student will not be able to move back into a place of learning. He will only escalate, and probably escalate his way out of the classroom. The teacher could, however, respond quietly, "I can see you're having a difficult morning. I'm going to set this pencil here, and I'll check on you in a minute." Then, WALK AWAY. After the student has had time to shift back out of "fight mode" and detect the teacher as an ally and not a threat, the teacher can then talk to the student about what is going on, and teach them correct response mechanisms. More importantly, the affective filter has been lowered, and the student can be open to learning.

In Scenario 3, while you, as the teacher, may be able to operate "by the seat of your pants," your struggling students will not be able to jump in and out of learning as quickly as you want them to. If there is chaos for the first three minutes of class, you have to assume that it will take another few minutes for your students to be ready to learn. Chaos causes the affective filter to rise, and it can take a few minutes to lower it and get their brains ready to work.

We will revisit many of these suggestions for lowering the affective filter in other parts of this book, because they are crucial components for setting up learning and creating independent learners in a culturally responsive classroom.

Learned Helplessness

According to Martin Seligman (2006), learned helplessness is the student's belief that he has no control over his ability to improve as a learner.[5] This is a very hopeless state that comes from continued failure and negative feedback. This is actually a survival mechanism of the brain to protect itself from the continued negative stimuli, and it typically manifests itself in students we see in "shut-down" mode.

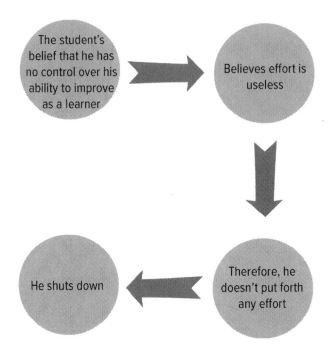

When we see students who have the behaviors of learned helplessness, we, as the teacher, can respond in one of two ways. We can recognize that it is a subconscious reaction and work towards building self-efficacy and an independent learner. Our other option is to see it as a lack of motivation, laziness or a behavior problem, and either ignore the student or address it with consequences. Which response has a better chance of facilitating learning?

The Learner's Brain

Let's now look at the brain from the learner's perspective.

The hippocampus is sometimes referred to as "the Dictionary." This is the memory system. The goal is to get new learning to the

hippocampus. Building background is key to making the connections needed to get the new information to "stick" in the hippocampus. So, how does this happen?

At the risk of oversimplifying, let's take a look at this process by starting with the part of the brain called the neocortex. The neocortex is made up of neuroplasticity, which is the "capacity of neurons and neural networks in the brain to change their connections and behavior in response to new information, sensory stimulation development, damage or dysfunction."[6]

In other words, this means the brain is always changing in response to our continued learning. Neurons gather to create a neural pathway when new learning is taking place. The more repetition and usage, the deeper the groove in the neural pathway, and the more the learning "sticks." When new information or experiences occur, neurons start firing off and connect. These are called **synaptic connections**. In response to cognitive challenges, problem-solving, and even increased physical activity (here's your plug for exercising!) synaptic connections are made, but only for a brief connection. The caveat to these synaptic connections is that if they are not used, they disconnect![3] Don't worry, we can relearn, but this is why usage, repetition, and connection to previous learning and experiences are so important.

Here are some more interesting facts about the brain and memory. Two types of long-term memory that we want to focus on here are taxon memory (primarily lists and facts—memory that moves into long-term memory after repetition) and locale memory (contextual and survival-oriented).[7]

Taxon memory is structured to remember lists, such as the alphabet, the causes of the Civil War, or the order of the planets in the

solar system. "Such memories move into long-term storage only after repeated rehearsal, and the motivation to remember is extrinsic—for example, grades, money or rewards."[7] Taxon memory is typically more difficult to move to the long-term memory storage.

Locale memory is made in context, intrinsic, typically sensory, and guided by our need to understand the world around us. Locale memory is much easier to move into long-term memory.

Locale Memory	Taxon Memory
Information gained in context	Structured lists
Motivated intrinsically by our need to understand	Information to be memorized
Easier to move into long-term memory	Motivated extrinsically (for example, grades)
	Typically more difficult to move into long-term memory

After looking at these two types of memory, how would we want to structure and facilitate most of our instruction—using locale memory or taxon memory? Locale memory, of course!

This knowledge brings us back to the importance of building background—connecting new information that could potentially be in our taxon memory to memories already formed as locale memory (prior experiences). This connection is fiercely powerful in creating real learning, especially when we think about our students who may not be as motivated extrinsically by grades.

Let's look at an example. Let's say you are a science teacher about to teach the process of photosynthesis. This is a very heavy vocabulary lesson! Before you jump into the terms of photosynthesis (which, let's be honest, may or may not be super intriguing to your 8th graders), let's set up this situation.

> "Ok class, everyone close your eyes. I want you to imagine that it is a beautiful, sunny day and you are doing your favorite activity outside. What are you doing? Playing soccer, football, playing in the park. Ok, got it? (This invokes a feeling through the senses.) Now, I want you to imagine that you wake up tomorrow, and there are no more plants. There is nothing green. No grass, no trees, no flowers, no gardens, no fields. Nothing. There is only concrete and buildings. What does it look like? How do you feel? How would this change your life?
>
> Write for three minutes.
>
> Now, share with a partner.
>
> Now, let's learn how plants stay alive, and what is the real benefit to us as humans!"

Do you see how we have taken what would go into taxon memory (vocabulary and the process of photosynthesis) and we have connected it to locale memory (the feeling of being outside)? This helps students move the new learning into long-term memory more easily, and when it is connected to an emotion, a deeper sense of learning occurs. This five minute building background activity is so powerful for the learning of new content.

Chapter 2 At a Glance

- The brain has two main functions: To protect and learn.
- The teacher has the power and responsibility to lower the affective filter in order to increase learning and language acquisition.
  - Create a positive environment.
  - Provide appropriate supports and scaffolds.
  - Provide relevant tasks.
  - Provide clear directions.
  - Provide order.
- Connecting taxon and locale memory increases real learning that can be applied in other situations.

Let's Process

1. How have you intentionally lowered the affective filter in your classroom? What do you do naturally to lower the affective filter? What do you need to be more intentional about?

2. How does this knowledge of the learning brain change your thoughts about instruction and your students?

3. Are there new concepts that you have previously taught by relying on the taxon memory that you could shift the instruction to lean on the locale memory?

4. Do each of your students KNOW that you want them in your class?

5. Do you create an environment that you would want your student learning in?

Strategies for Implementation

Strategies for lowering the affective filter:

- Create a positive environment
  - team building activities
  - individual handshakes/greetings
- Post directions, especially during transition times (beginning of class, change of tasks, end of class, etc.)
- Ask yourself, "Does this task directly link to learning?"

Suggestions for scaffolds:

- Provide sentence frames
- Provide word banks
- Use total physical response (TPR) to connect a hand motion to a meaning
- Use repetition—chorally and individually
- Chunk texts, directions, and content

Favorite Resources on This Topic

The Learning Brain, Eric Jenson[8]

Stra-tiques: Strategies and Activities for the English Learner, EL Saber Enterprises[9]

Kagan Cooperative Learning, Dr. Spencer Kagan[10]

PART II
The Whom

"Every student can learn, just not on the same day or in the same way."

GEORGE EVANS

*T*he goal of culturally responsive teaching is to provide equity for all students, but for many of us, we come from a very different cultural perspective than our students. In the next two chapters, we are going to dive into different groups of students—students of color, specifically Latino and African American students, Long-Term English Learners and students of poverty (who come from a variation of ethnic backgrounds). As we discuss these groups, we can't possibly sum up every person within these groups, simply some general characteristics.

CHAPTER 3

Teaching by Reaching All Students

"The promise of a better tomorrow ain't never reached me,

plus my teachers were too petrified in class to teach me."

— Never B Peace Lyrics, Tupac Shakur[1]

*a*s in every good practice of pedagogy, knowing our students is a key factor in building and facilitating instruction that results in learning. Getting to know them on a personal level by discovering their hobbies, family life, goals, and personalities is important for building that connection that students from a collectivist background need from their teachers. However, if we really want to be a culturally responsive teacher, it's imperative to understand the cultural and circumstantial perspective that our students are using to view the world.

Once we understand the cultural lens behind the behaviors and responses of these students, we will be much more able to connect with them on the level that actually brings change.

As we dive into the next discussion of who our students are and where they are coming from, please know that this section comes from a place of love and desperation. For years I loved and taught my students as best I knew how. But I didn't reach them on the level they deserved, because I didn't really *know* them. In these next two chapters, we will dive into specific groups of students who are struggling across the nation. We will look at how our systems—be it on a grand scale or even the systems we set up in our classroom—have to be set up to meet the needs of *all* of our students.

Cornelius Minor profoundly states that, "Our journey starts with an understanding that no great good can be done for a people if we do not listen to them first. Powerful teaching is rooted in powerful listening."[2]

The first fact we have to accept is that the school system in the United States is not reaching these marginalized groups of students. Every student is *not* given a fair shot at education. All schools and teachers are *not* created equally, and the quality of education a student receives is often dependent on where they live. This can be defined as *structural racism*.

Structural racism is a very current and real racial divide that is still very much alive today. Because of the way our society is set up, there is a direct relationship between where one lives and "how location and geography affects one's access to education and job opportunities, as well as other quality-of-life factors"[3] that we must choose to no longer overlook. Hammond addresses this so beautifully as it relates to education:

"Over time, because of structural racialization in education, we have seen a new type of intellectual apartheid happening in schools, creating dependent learners who cannot access

the curriculum and independent learners who have had the opportunity to build the cognitive skills to do the deep learning on their own. Rather than stepping back, looking at the ways we structure inequity in education, and interrupting these practices, we simply focus on creating short-term solutions to get dependent students of color to score high on each year's standardized tests. We don't focus on building their intellective capacity so that they can begin to fill their own learning gaps with proper scaffolding."[3]

In other words—not every student has an equal opportunity, and the quicker that we recognize this, the quicker we can start remedying the situation. Here's part of the problem, if I may be blunt. For those of us who live in middle-upper-class American neighborhoods, we may never see this structural racialization. We may honestly never know it exists. But it does.

In *Teaching Reading to Black Adolescent Males*, Dr. Alfred Tatum clearly portrays the ongoing battle through the lens of literacy for these students dealing with the element of poverty.

The National Assessment of Education Progress (NAEP) indicates a correlation between low levels of reading achievement and socioeconomic status. Poor students at grades 4, 8, and 12 are underperforming in reading when compared to students who are not poor. This is particularly salient when black males are considered. The reading achievement gaps are wider among adolescents. Many black male high school graduates are reading at the same level as white middle school students

or below. Many of these black students attend low-achieving schools staffed with underqualified teachers who are unable to address their students' literacy needs. Also, many of these students' teachers have low expectations about their students' ability to meet high academic standards.[1]

A child who is born in a high-crime, low-income area typically has a choice of one school. That school is often staffed with inexperienced teachers and ineffective administrators. It is filled with children and youth that are living in survival mode, with daily situations that most of us, and my own child, will never experience. They are bringing adult issues such as crime, domestic abuse, instability, and a fear of the loss of basic needs such as food, clothing and shelter to school daily, to teachers and administrators untrained and unequipped to bring learning through these issues and help these students rise above. The dropout rates and failure rates paint this picture all too clearly.

But let's take this a step further. Many of these students are sitting in our classrooms sprinkled amongst students who've never feared for their life, been a victim of a crime, or been needy of the basic essentials in life. These precious students are expected to think and work the same as a student who is clothed, fed and lives day-to-day in a world of stability and comfort. How can we not see that we will have to meet the needs of each of these student groups differently?

"Racial Amnesia"

As a middle-class Caucasian living in a middle-class society, I believe it was subconsciously engrained in me to be "color-blind," because to talk about differences or color could be offensive.

But to *NOT* talk about differences or color is offensive.

When I said phrases like, "I don't even see color. I love all of my students the same. I teach all of my students the same. All of my students are given the same instruction and therefore given the same opportunities—some just don't choose to take them."—I am in essence saying, "I see all of my students the same as me—white. So I will teach all of my students as if they come from the same cultural and economic background as myself. And if they don't get the instruction, that's because they chose not to."

Dyson (2001) has dubbed the lack of attention on the present condition of students of color "racial amnesia."[4] In thinking specifically of African American males, Tatum states, "The failure of institutions to acknowledge or adequately respond to the needs of black males, instead blaming these youths for what is really the institutions' own failure, has caused black youths to respond to turmoil in their own way."[1] We just can't move through education blindly and expect every student to grab hold of the content in a meaningful way.

So, let's dive in and learn about these precious students we have the honor of serving.

The history and learning styles of African Americans

To the African American culture, their historical journey plays an important role in how they learn and grow and view their role in society today. This cannot be discounted. A strong emphasis on a family or group dynamic, a need to feel or seem in control of the present situation, and a heavy emphasis on movement and rhythm are all factors that contribute to the African American perspective. Tileston and Darling (2008) put forth some interesting facts:

Male African-American children are 5x more likely than male Anglo-American children to initiate conversations with others, to act out to get attention, or to move around the classroom.

Many African American students express their personalities, movement, and body style through their walk, hair and dress, and during games and dance through a love for rhythm.[5]

Let's connect movement to learning and let them use what drives them to make the connections to content!

Many of the African American students in our classrooms pay more attention to the people in their environment than the objects or things. Because of this, they are better able to distinguish emotions, recognize faces, and pick up on nuances in social situations.[5]

Relationships must be genuine. These students will quickly pick up on inauthenticity! They cannot be fooled by the teacher. They are keenly aware of how the teacher is thinking or feeling towards the class, and this will often dictate the students' level of trust with the teacher. As teachers, we need to genuinely connect with these students, and have authentic conversations and experiences with them.

> Students have a response style that leans more towards extroversion than introversion. They get their energy from, and direct their actions toward, other people as a means of self-expression.[5]

These students will have a tendency to respond outwardly. This tells us that we need to teach appropriate ways to discuss and debate! They want to be engaged, and the energy they get often stems from interactions with their peers! We can use this to promote learning in such powerful ways!

> African American children tend to use different categories than European Americans to sort and organize information. The learning tasks need to be relevant to their current experience of reality.[5]

Minor (2017) describes how having conversations with his students moved him toward realizing that listening to children is one of the most powerful things a teacher can do. By listening carefully, Cornelius discovered that his "lessons were not, at all, linked to that student's reality."[1]

"Research on cognitive processing styles indicates that African Americans are more likely to consider information in a holistic, relational, and field-dependent manner than are Anglo-Europeans."[5]

In other words, "busy-work" and decontextualized content will not be found meaningful because these students' leverage for learning is in the value and relevancy of the content, not in the grade they will receive upon completion of the task.

What do these statements tell us? In the classroom, we can best focus student attention if they are in groups focused on interaction with opportunities to process information aloud with others. They tend to be better at holistic thinking and synthesizing as opposed to learning in logical or sequential order. They do better with looking at the "big picture" and need to know how the learning is relevant to their current situation. They thrive on interactions with others, and will have these interactions regardless of whether or not we facilitate them, so we might as well embed them in our instruction to increase learning and provide an outlet for this energy. And we need to provide opportunities in the classroom for movement and dance. The more we can connect this to learning, the more learning will occur!

AFRICAN AMERICAN STUDENTS IN POVERTY

As with any ethnic group, living in poverty brings an additional set of challenges. In the next chapter, we will dive further into the mindset of students of poverty, but I do want to address some specific character

traits of African American children and youth living in generational poverty.

For African Americans living in generational poverty, turmoil is often the norm. Turmoil in the community, in the family unit, and even intrinsically, is the daily struggle. We've already stated how the learning must be relevant, and for students living in turmoil, they must see how the learning can affect change to move them out of the present state of turmoil. Tatum (2015) states, "Black males are increasingly skeptical that education can help them escape from their low economic strata. Many of these young men believe that their fate has been determined and that failure in inevitable. The turmoil in their lives is so intense they are unable to see beyond it, and they do not believe anyone cares for them."[1]

They see people in their neighborhoods who have graduated and still live in a state of turmoil. Graduation, and the grades needed to get to graduation, are often not the leverage points that motivate these students. Understanding the *why* and gaining the thinking and problem-solving skills necessary to be independent learners starts the process of rising above their circumstances.

It is also important to understand the behavior of many of these students, particularly the African American males, as they navigate their day-to-day lives in survival mode. "Conflict often exists between institutions and black males because those in the establishment lack understanding, or misunderstand, the cultural-specific behaviors exhibited by black males."[1]

One survival technique that Tatum mentions is the 'Cool Pose,' which is the use of behaviors, phrases, physical posturing, and carefully crafted performances to convey a strong impression of pride,

strength and control. This coping mechanism is often used to hide self-doubt, insecurity (particularly in the school setting) and the inner turmoil that these students carry around.

While this 'Cool Pose' may help these students coast socially, there are many negative consequences associated with this behavior because the 'Cool Pose':

- Hinders potential and growth because of a fear of failure that taking a risk in a new experience may bring (in this case—learning)

- Brings trouble with authorities based on a refusal to break the cool pose and a misunderstanding of the behavior from the authorities

- Prevents receiving support because of the inclination to disclose little about himself

- Causes the student to avoid institutions that are deemed "uncool"—schools, museums, churches—that could actually help them alleviate their turmoil[1]

How does understanding this posture help us, as teachers, reach these students in the classroom? We can't change their circumstances or even their response to their circumstances, but we can reach them where they are. We can help them gain actual control of their learning to help them feel more in control of their future. We can avoid embarrassing them at all costs, and connect with them on a deeper level. We can avoid using phrases like, "You need to do this work to pass" and create meaningful connections to their present lives.

We can detach ourselves from this behavior and not take it

personally so we avoid reacting emotionally when their responses to challenges in the classroom are not what we deem appropriate. Understanding where the posture stems from can help us in viewing the student through a more accurate lens.

Another common response to the constant turmoil so many of these students face is anger. We see this in a lot of the music and media that many of these students are immersed in. The popular gangsta rap genre graphically depicts the feelings of this group caught in the cycle of turmoil.

Unfortunately, schools and teachers inadvertently perpetuate the anger and learning difficulties for African Americans in turmoil. Tatum outlines a few of these causes.

- Micro-aggression: Things teachers say on a day-to-day basis that anger their black students and project stereotypical images, such as:

  - "I'm not going to let you play basketball if you don't do your work."

  - "If you practiced your math as much as you practiced your rappin', you wouldn't be failing."[1]

- Psychometric warfare: Teachers use test data to determine the intelligence level of their students and therefore reduce the difficult problems black students face into intellectually simplistic descriptions. This practice, while being done with the intentions of 'filling in the gaps' for students and teaching them on their level, lowers the rigor and keeps these students from gaining the cognitive skills they need to reach higher expectations.

- Misguided educational placements: Educators sometimes choose to place black males in special classes rather than develop culturally appropriate practices to help in their education. Black males, specifically, are often found in lower academic tracks, again hindering their potential and growth.

- Barriers to learning: Schools and growth tracks often consist of poorly prepared teachers, inadequate educational facilities, low teacher expectations and ineffective administrators.

- Expulsion and suspension: The rates of these punishments are disproportionately higher than all other subpopulations.[1]

Clearly, there are some very real challenges that our students are facing, and some very real needs that we can meet.

Latinos/Mexican-Americans

While many of the Latino cultures share very similar characteristics, it is significant to note that there are many Latino students from countries other than Mexico. We will be discussing both the Latino culture in general, and specific characteristics of Mexican-Americans.

When looking at the learning styles of many of these students from these collectivist cultures, we know that they value and appreciate relationships. They will learn best when material has social content, and when they can collaborate to build on and learn content. Ramirez and Casteneda (1974) and Gay (2000, 2002) believe that

many Mexican-American children are field-dependent, that is, they perceive globally and experience new information holistically.[5] This goes back to needing a relevant, "big picture" lesson, and not just decontextualized vocabulary or lessons.

Language is a crucial component for understanding and valuing this culture. "Villegas (1991), Kagan and Zahn (1975), and Shade, Kelly and Oberg (1997) have all suggested that we cannot understand the culture of Mexican-Americans without understanding the significance of their language. For our Hispanic children, the Spanish language represents their heritage and culture; in many cases the primary means by which they communicate their feelings."[5] When we diminish or devalue this language or mode of communication, we are, in fact, communicating that we devalue their culture. While it is imperative we teach the English language, we also have to do so in a way that still values their first language. Saying phrases like, "No Spanish! English only!" or "I don't want to hear that language in here. I speak English, so there should only be English spoken in my class!" can devalue the language in an unnecessary way.

The Mexican-American community is often faced with an ongoing internal dilemma—assimilation and acculturation to the United States verses maintaining the culture and language of their native land. If we want to be culturally responsive, we need to help our students maintain their identity with their cultural *and* ethnic backgrounds <u>and</u> develop their identity as Americans. Students shouldn't have to choose, but they need to know that their culture and language is valued, just as the culture and English language is valued. It's not one or the other.

It's important to note, "even though Spanish is one of the world's greatest languages and ranks second among languages most spoken

in America, it has a low prestige in most of the United States."[5] How do you view the Spanish language? Is it something you value, or is it something you discourage?

Here are some ways to value the language:

1. Have the students teach you some words that are applicable to your content.

2. Ask students to describe specific texts or ideas in Spanish. For example:

    a. "How do you say, "Great job!" in Spanish?" (Then you can use this affirmation.)

    b. "What word would you use to describe this character in Spanish? Ok, now translate to English so I know what it means."

    c. Write the Spanish and English word on the Word Wall for vocabulary instruction.

3. Explain the process of language acquisition and help the students set goals for building their own second language.

On an academic note, research has shown that the more students develop their social and academic language in their first language, the easier and deeper they will develop it in their second language. So again, it doesn't have to be one or the other.

Another characteristic to consider is, because of their strong family ties and respect for and obedience to elders, Latino students tend to internalize criticism from their teachers and elders. This is valuable information in knowing how to relate, respond and give feedback to this group.

While our next group certainly encompasses more than one cultural and ethnic segment, it is often found within the Latino student group.

Preventing, Reaching and Moving Long-Term English Learners

As the population of ELs continues to grow in the United States, firm processes and strategies have to be put into place to meet their academic needs. Between the 2009–2010 and 2014–15 school years, the percentage of EL students increased in more than half of the states in the United States, with increases of over 40% in five states.[6] These students are often bright overcomers who are fully capable of meeting the challenges of school and life and will excel with the right approach.

However, when that doesn't happen, and these students fall through the proverbial cracks in the education system, they become Long-Term ELs ("LTELs"). There is never a good reason to be a LTEL. Having this label alone means that the student is not where he or she should be and is not on track. Academically, LTELs tend to struggle with acquiring new academic vocabulary and literacy in their second language. In addition, there are social and emotional issues that ensue that make the learning nearly impossible—until you, as the culturally responsive teacher, come along.

Understanding the battle these students are facing, embracing the culture that encompasses every part of them, and then bridging the learning to make self-sufficient, independent learners is (and should be) every teacher's dream. In this section, we are going to learn

how to love these kids into learning within an environment that sets them up for success and expectations they must rise to, along with the linguistic supports and scaffolds they need to be successful.

The Reasons

What creates LTELs? Why is there such an epidemic of underperforming ELs when we have extensive research proving that these kids can actually be some of our most successful students with the right instruction? Do we, as native English speakers, have any effect on these students?

Of course we do! We have to get to know our students!

Who are LTELs? These are students who have been in the country for six years or more and are still labeled "English Learners" because they have not met the linguistic or academic standards set forth by the government. In Texas, in 2015, there were more than 500,000 English learners, Kindergarten – 12th grade, with 25% of those students being Long-Term ELs. Because LTELs are not labeled as such until they have been in the country at least six years, the majority of LTELs are at the secondary level. At most secondary campuses, the majority of the English learners will be Long-Term ELs. This is particularly frustrating because this is a completely preventable problem!

In addition to LTELs wreaking havoc on a district's accountability measures, there are far greater consequences (in my opinion) when we look at the affect being a LTEL has on a student.

Before we dive into the issues with LTELs, I want to explain the two types of LTELs we typically encounter: 1) students who were

born in the US, and 2) students who were born in their native countries and immigrated over at a young age.

Students born in the United States are considered "first generation" if their parents were born in their native country. When these students enter a school district in Kindergarten, they are given a home-language survey. If the parents mark that the primary language spoken at home is a language other than English, in most states, students are assessed and then placed into either a bilingual or ESL program. The circumstance that we find with first generation kids is that they often times do not develop their L1 (first language) or their L2 (second language—in most cases, English) fluently in an academic manner. To compound this issue, we as teachers may miss this completely, because the students speak fluently in English *socially*, which is very different from *academic* language.

If you have students in your class who fall under the "first generation" umbrella, they probably embody a lot of the American culture, speak English fluently (maybe even without an accent), but shut down or act out when asked to do academic tasks. Sometimes, we have a tendency to look at this as a behavior or motivation issue, when, in fact, it is actually a language issue.

The other group of LTELs are the students who immigrated to the United States at a young age, but have been in US schools for more than six years and have been unable to exit the program by whatever criteria the state has set. These students often look the same as the first-generation students, being fluent in social language, but struggling with the academic language.

So, what happens? I've narrowed it down to three primary issues these students face—the three Ls.

1. Lack of intentional, ongoing language building

2. Language plateau

3. Learned helplessness

Lack of Intentional, Ongoing Language Building

English learners should be monitored each year and measured for their linguistic progress. In my research, we typically see the gap begin around their third year in the country. The issue we find is that there is not enough of a "red flag" for a real sense of urgency to fill the gap in their linguistic progress, especially with general education teachers who may not be especially educated in linguistic proficiency. In other words, if the student is doing "okay for an EL" in third grade, but has not made the progress expected, he will still go to the fourth grade as an EL. Unfortunately, at the end of fourth grade, that teacher may have the same comment as the third-grade teacher, but the gap continues to grow. Academic vocabulary isn't built, reading comprehension isn't developed, and then by the time the student gets into middle school, he is now a LTEL. At this point, his academic progress slows tremendously.

Another issue we find is that because the student is proficient in social language, linguistic accommodations and scaffolds are not put into place to teach academic content and new vocabulary. Let's take a moment to talk about language. When we are talking about language acquisition, we focus on two types of language—Basic Interpersonal Communication Skills (BICS) and Cognitive Academic Language Proficiency (CALP). BICS refers to social language, the everyday

language we use to communicate. CALP refers to academic language, and the ability to acquire new academic language or vocabulary.[7] If a student is on track, it takes anywhere from one to three years to develop their BICS fluently. However, it takes 5–10 years to develop CALP fluently, and that is if the student is making the appropriate progress.

The teacher often blames behavior, a lack of caring or motivation, or another academic issue for the lack of academic achievement, when actually language development is the primary culprit.

Language Plateau

Another very real issue is the language plateau that is almost unavoidable. There is a natural growth early on in language acquisition when a student who speaks another language is in a primarily English-speaking environment. However, if language acquisition isn't intentionally taught, a plateau, or language block, will occur.

Potential ways to overcome the language block
1. Set clear goals
2. Use authentic material
3. Focus on problem areas
4. Learn more vocabulary
5. Interact in English
6. Build confidence[8]

As always, we shift this to your classroom. What does it look like to intentionally help your students overcome their language plateau?

SET CLEAR GOALS

Goal setting is always a meaningful practice when trying to move forward, and it is no different in building language. In Texas, educators have the English Language Proficiency Standards (ELPS), which very clearly lay out language goals for students. In the rest of the United States, 40 other states and territories participate in the WIDA Consortium. WIDA contains the student Can-Do statements that also lay out very clear language goals. Being familiar with these goals as a teacher, as well as setting common language goals with your students, will be very beneficial in moving students over the plateau.

USE AUTHENTIC MATERIAL

Language is built more concretely and easily when the meanings in a new language can connect to the meanings in a previously learned language. For this reason, providing authentic material for students to use while building their language is highly effective. We know that students need to read, write, speak and listen in English to be considered fluent. When they can read, write, speak and listen about content that is relevant to their lives and learning, this can be a very powerful connection. While at times it is appropriate to lower the reading level in order to build comprehension, giving a 10th grader a third grade text written on third grade content is not appropriate.

FOCUS ON PROBLEM AREAS

Language building is intentional. When we have set specific goals, we can then measure the progress. Once we are measuring the progress, we can recognize specific areas where there is a deficit. When we identify the problem areas, we can work with students to intentionally build the language in this area. Some common, recurring problem areas to be aware of are:

- Subject-verb agreement

- Past and present tenses

- Narrating or describing in writing

- Sentence structures

LEARN MORE VOCABULARY

You've probably noticed that this is a recurring concept. Vocabulary has such an impact on comprehension (some say up to 97%), that intentional vocabulary instruction is necessary for building language and content. We discuss vocabulary in other chapters in this book, but when we are discussing building vocabulary specifically for overcoming the language plateau, here are some strategies to consider:

Vocabulary Strategies for Overcoming the Language Plateau

Teach multi-meaning words.

Make vocabulary visual in the classroom.

Have students repeat vocabulary words and meanings as often as possible.

Have students learn vocabulary through the 4 domains: reading, writing, listening and speaking.

Teach vocabulary explicitly *and* in context.

Show video, pictures, symbols or realia (real items) whenever possible to teach vocabulary.

INTERACT IN ENGLISH

This may seem basic, but we need to facilitate and plan conversations in English, even social conversations. Having conversations with the students as they enter the classroom, allowing students to speak socially to each other in English during a structured conversation time, and using the vocabulary in conversation is crucial for getting over the language plateau. I know we often feel like there is not time for these conversations, but I would submit to you that you will be repaid in academic time when students have an increased understanding of the language when you facilitate the three minutes of a structured social conversation consistently.

BUILD CONFIDENCE

Building confidence is a direct result of creating a safe climate in your classroom. When students feel safe enough to take a risk, whether

it be in learning or language, they will feel more intrinsic success. This success leads to self-efficacy, and this leads to confidence. If the environment is not set up in this way, students will stay quiet or shut down, and their language will surely stay on the plateau.

Question stems and response frames are also terrific ways to build the student's confidence while they are speaking or writing about content. These are scaffolds in that as the student's language and confidence is built, the frames can be removed.

Another great strategy is choral repetition. When a new or important concept is introduced, facilitating choral repetition, where the entire class repeats a word or meaning several times, lowers the risk factor for the student and gives them an opportunity to practice speaking and pronouncing the word several times.

Overcoming the language plateau is intentional, but doable!

Will you help students get over this plateau?

Preventing Long-Term ELs

Let's take another step backwards. Before we continue to work with Long-Term ELs, let's look at how to *prevent* LTELs. Building language must be explicit and intentional. Students will most likely be able to pick up on BICS by being immersed in an English rich environment, but the CALP requires more intention. Students must have linguistic accommodations in order to simultaneously build language and content. What does it mean to *build language*?

Here's a quick lesson in language. There are four language domains that most people recognize: reading, writing, listening and speaking. A student must be fluent in all four language domains in order to be

fluent in a language. As teachers, no matter what content or grade level we teach, if we have ELs, we must be intentional about building all four language domains in our content. If you teach science, students need to be writing about science, discussing science, listening and repeating science vocabulary, and reading about science. If you teach math, students need to be explaining how to solve a problem and why they chose that problem-solving method, listening to you and peers explain the math vocabulary, read the steps, and write their thoughts. You get the idea. If students are to learn new academic vocabulary, and build language at the same time, they must be reading about it, writing about it, speaking about it and listening and responding to it. This must be done on an ongoing and consistent basis.

Here is the other concept to think about: linguistic accommodations and scaffolds. The goal of teaching English learners is to help them access grade level content. Two ways to do this are through linguistic accommodations and scaffolds. Although these terms are sometimes used interchangeably, linguistic accommodations are language supports that decrease the language barrier English learners experience when learning and demonstrating knowledge and skills in English. Here are some common linguistic accommodations:

- Visuals
- Hand motions/total physical response
- Repetition of words
- Bilingual dictionary
- Peer support
- Extra time

Scaffolds are put into place to support the content. The goal of these scaffolds is to allow the student to access the content. Here are some examples of common scaffolds:

- Sentence frames
- Chunking instruction or reading
- Wait time to process questions
- Graphic organizers

Linguistic accommodations and scaffolds *are not optional* for English learners in their first five years of being in US schools. While it is up to the teacher to determine which scaffolds and accommodations are appropriate for each student based on their proficiency levels and their learning styles, they are necessary.

The problem we see time and time again is that students will build their BICS language quickly. To a teacher who is not educated in language acquisition, they sometimes think that language is no longer an issue and the need to intentionally build and provide accommodations and scaffolds is no longer there. These supports are pulled from the students too early, and their language development begins to plateau, bringing us back to the issues we brought to light at the beginning of the chapter.

NOW, let's determine what to do when we have LTELs sitting in your classroom.

EL Saber Enterprises recommends working with your LTELs using the acronym VOICE. See the chart on the next page.

Visuals: Word walls, anchor charts, pictures, realia (real items), and videos are used to build vocabulary, background, and comprehension.

Oracy: "The ability to express oneself fluently and grammatically correct,"[9] academic dialogue, speaking about specific content.

Interactive Vocabulary: Specifically and intentionally facilitating students to interact with vocabulary terms through conversation, games, and manipulation of words and meanings.

Comprehension: Understanding new information (orally or through text) in a given content area.

Evaluation of Language: Both the teacher and the student have clear targets to reach based on language goals, and evaluate these regularly.

USED WITH PERMISSION FROM EL SABER ENTERPRISES.

V is for Visuals. It is so crucial to give students visuals when introducing new vocabulary, connecting to old vocabulary, or trying to increase comprehension. Word Walls, anchor charts, pictures, realia (real items), and videos are all examples of ways to use visuals.

O is for Oracy. Oracy is the "ability to express oneself fluently and grammatically correct."[9] This skill, and the practice of this skill, is so critical to LTELs learning the content. Students must have the opportunity to discuss through the use of a new vocabulary and content. "Sit and Get" simply will not work for your Long-Term English Learners. There is very little language (if any) built when

students are copying notes down from a PowerPoint. They are not able to process the content, make connections, or formulate ideas. Most of them won't be able to tell you the last word they wrote down. They need to have the opportunity to discuss the content if language and learning is going to take place.

I is for Interactive Vocabulary. A lack of vocabulary is the reason for the majority of academic issues for your Long-Term ELs. As previously discussed, writing down the definition is going to do very little for building language or learning. They must interact with the vocabulary, look at the word parts, play games, classify the words, talk about the words, use the words in context, and make connections. This must be built into the instruction. We will talk more about vocabulary and some strategies for classroom implementation Chapter 7.

C is for Comprehension. We have to make sure our LTELs are comprehending. They need to be comprehending text, instruction, information, and directions. If we are not checking for understanding and determining on an ongoing basis what the level of comprehension is for our LTELs, we will lose many of them along the way. The linguistic accommodations and scaffolds mentioned previously directly tie to their comprehension of the grade-level material. There are also strategies for increasing comprehension. (See Strategies for Classroom Implementation in the Voice Chart in the Appendix.)

E is for Evaluation of Language. With many of our LTELS, they have been in the program so long that to the student, their data is no longer meaningful. Many of them will even tell you "I didn't even

know I was an English learner!" It is difficult to set goals and make progress without having a clear idea of where you currently are. The importance of conferencing with these students, putting an emphasis on their language proficiency, and setting some clear goals for what they will be working on cannot be undermined. This allows you and the student to work together for a common goal, and this goes hand in hand with culturally responsive teaching![10]

Learned Helplessness

We discussed this occurrence in Chapter 2, and it will be mentioned again in Chapter 4, but it cannot be overlooked. If the students have reached this point of hopelessness from years and years of failing and not progressing, we can put all of the strategies in place that we want, but we will have to address the emotional support as well.

How do we overcome this learned helplessness, specifically with LTELs?

- Build a relationship.

- Set measurable goals for you and the student to meet together—build an alliance.

- Provide supports and scaffolds that allow the students to think for themselves and have success.

- Understand the cultural lens in which the students are viewing school and become an ally.

So let's talk about solutions!

One of the key beliefs that a culturally responsive teacher must have is the firm belief that all students can and will achieve academically. They just have to be willing to approach the learning in different ways.

Geneva Gay, one of the pioneers in culturally responsive teaching, asserts that "building a relationship anchored in affirmation, mutual respect, and validation is the key that breeds an unshakable belief that marginalized students not only can, but also will, improve their school achievement."[3] When I first read this, it shook me deep down to my core. I always had good relationships with my students, and I loved them, no doubt. But I didn't *really* know them. I still looked at them through my own lens, which brought such a disconnect to my students who viewed the world out of a different cultural lens.

Gay affirms the idea that when we get to know our students on a deeper level, and we build the relationship that both the teacher and the students so desperately need, only then will we *truly know* their potential, and know that even through the struggles they face, they are more than competent and capable to achieve academically with the right kind of instruction. It's not a superficial cheer that says, "You can do it!" It's an *unshakeable* belief. Teachers must believe in the students' ability to achieve—that even when a student responds in anger, or postures up in the cool pose, teachers don't give up. Instead, we take a step back and reflect on our own practices and responses. And we continue to hold expectations high, make relevant and valuable connections to the current world they live in, and build solid relationships that are fostered on trust and mutual respect.

We must help students build resilience.

Teachers must establish caring relationships, hold high expectations for every student and provide opportunities for student participation and contribution. Building resilience is a key factor for influencing independent learners.

Key characteristics of a resilient student

A good, strong sense of selflessness, or giving of one's self

The possessing of life skills, such as good decision-making, self-control, and assertiveness

An ability to be sociable

A sense of humor

An internal locus of control

Autonomy

Orientation toward a positive future

Adaptability and flexibility

An interest in and connection to learning

Self-motivation

Personal competence in one or multiple areas

Some element of self-worth or self-efficacy[11]

Understanding this list can help us build resiliency for our students. The teacher must value and teach each of these characteristics in order to instill the resilience our students desperately need to achieve ongoing academic success. Building the students' personal competency by having them set goals and self-monitor, creating relevant lessons with challenging student tasks, and facilitating a tribal community

within the classroom climate where students help and cheer for each other, are all ways to start the process of building resiliency.

Tileston and Darling cite research, focused on Latino and African American students who were poor and successful in school, that identified educational resilience as a primary factor in their success. "Teachers (build resiliency) by creating a culturally responsive classroom environment, attend to the learning process, and contextualize the content and modifying the products for students to demonstrate their learning."[5]

Hopefully you now have a clearer understanding of these specific groups, as well as some ideas for moving forward. We will dig into more solutions for building a culturally responsive classroom with high rigor and expectations in Part III of this book.

Chapter 3 At a Glance

- LTELs need specific language building through scaffolds and linguistic accommodations.

- VOICE is a great guide for reaching LTELs.

- Vocabulary must be taught explicitly.

Let's Process

1. Do you have Long-Term ELs? What is their current behavior or academic performance?

2. Are they a product of one of the 3 L's?

   a. Lack of intentional, ongoing language building,

   b. Language plateau, and

   c. Learned helplessness.

3. What are some ways that you can linguistically support these Long-Term ELs? Be specific!

Strategies for Implementation

VOICE Chart for working with and preventing LTELs — See Appendix

Favorite Resources on This Topic

Stra-tiques, EL Saber Enterprises[9]

DOK Question Stems and Response Frames, EL Saber Enterprises[13]

Academic Vocabulary for English Learners, EL Saber Enterprises[14]

CHAPTER 4

Facing and *Moving Past* the Unique Challenges of Students of Poverty

"Almost every student you meet might be fighting a battle you know nothing about. Stop. Think. Then make your response accordingly."[1]
— **Author Unknown**

*P*overty can be an invisible distractor from the day-to-day learning that needs to take place in a classroom. Just like teaching LTELs, students of poverty can often look and sound like any other student, making their struggles difficult to pin-point. I was recently working at a rural school with fifth and sixth grade teachers. This district is primarily Caucasian, with almost 70% of their students on free and reduced lunch in the fifth and sixth grade. I spent a few days going into each fifth and sixth grade ELA and Reading class. I made note of six students total who were clearly living in an environment of poverty. The rest of the students visually "fit in" with everyone else.

The problem, unfortunately, is that because of the generational poverty embedded in their reality, their brains don't operate like the middle-class student, and without understanding the differences, many of these students will not achieve the academic success they need to begin moving out of the cycle.

It is important to note that poverty is not a "culture." However, generational poverty has such a heavy influence on how the brain is wired that these students absolutely need a culturally responsive teacher. In this chapter, we will see how culturally responsive teaching is a solution for many of these students as well.

In *Teaching with Poverty in Mind (2009)*, Eric Jenson states that there are four primary risks associated with poverty. They are:

- Emotional and social challenges
- Acute and chronic stressors
- Cognitive lags
- Health and safety issues[2]

These are huge impactors, and as teachers, they cannot be overlooked in our instruction. The cycles that happen in families of generational poverty impact every part of the student, and we just can't expect them to learn the same way as others who are not facing the same situations.

"Common issues in low-income families include depression, chemical dependence, and hectic work schedules—all factors that interfere with the healthy attachments that foster children's self-esteem, sense of mastery of their environment, and optimistic attitudes. Instead, poor children often feel isolated and unloved, feelings that kick off a downward spiral of unhappy life events, including poor academic performance,

behavioral problems, dropping out of school, and drug abuse."[2]

Cause and Effect

The effects of poverty are widespread and comprehensive and start with infants. Let's take a look at the causes of the issues associated with poverty.

Parents caught in the cycle of generational poverty have their own struggles. Because we are talking about the effects of poverty, it's important to look at the root of the problems we see in school, and that often begins in infancy. Circumstances like teenage pregnancy, drug and alcohol abuse, depression and inadequate health care cause weak and insecure attachments between the mother and child as an infant.[2]

Issues Parents Face in Generational Poverty
• Teenage pregnancy
• Poor health care
• Drug and alcohol abuse
• Mental illness
• Overworked
• Constant stress

These attachment issues have consequences that follow the students as they grow older. Jenson states that research has found that to grow up emotionally healthy, children under three need:

- Strong, reliable primary caregiver

- Safe, predictable, stable environments

- 10–20 hours a week of *attunement*—warm, sensitive, harmonious, reciprocal interactions that help the infant develop a range of healthier emotions (which we will dive into a little later in this chapter under the six hard-wired traits)

- Enrichment through personalized, increasingly complex activities[2]

If these basic emotional needs are not met at a young age, children don't produce the brain cells needed for appropriate social and emotional development. This can already begin altering the course of their success in school and life.

Living in the cycle of poverty is often characterized by chronic stress. Many parents in poverty feel the brunt of this as they go through life overworked and overstressed. Because of these factors, parents in generational poverty tend to be more authoritative and absent, leaving children to spend time alone and often fend for themselves. These children tend to play outside less and are involved in fewer after-school activities.[3] This causes less opportunity to develop proper relationships or practice responding appropriately.

Overworked and overstressed people living in generational poverty have clearly not seen the benefit of their own education.

Getting an education or even graduating did not change their own circumstances; therefore, parents may also have a negative attitude towards school. This can lead to absenteeism with the student and a lack of parental involvement. This can also enhance the "school vs student" perspective that we may have to shift when these students enter our classrooms. Again, this all works into the system in which poverty lives.

In addition, children living in poverty often find themselves without a center of control. When there is no sense of control or stability at home, students often bring that sense of a loss of control into their lives at school. They feel like they do not have control over themselves or their performance. A lack of feeling of control completely destroys self-efficacy, which is the student's feeling that he has the resources or ability to achieve success or problem-solve. A lack of control moves the student completely into reactive mode, causing them to make impulsive decisions and react or respond inappropriately. This, again, is where we see learned helplessness set in.

Poverty and The Brain

Poverty changes the wiring of the brain. Many students in poverty live in a state of constant stress. Because many of them live in a place with chronic stressors (abuse, constant mobility and moving, unstable environments, unstable parents, substance abuse in the home), they haven't developed the correct response modes. When students live in constant survival mode, they don't ever settle in their place of homeostasis—where they feel at rest and peace. Even after a stressful day, most of us can go home to a relatively stress-free home, where

we have a good meal, a peaceful evening, and a good night's sleep. This restful time helps our brain reset and be more prepared to take on the next day. If we are enduring stress at work, and then go home to more stress at home, the wiring in our brain will begin to change, as we see happening in so many of these children.

Going back to our brain-based learning, stress produces a hormone called cortisol, and cortisol mostly affects the prefrontal cortex. Chronic stress diminishes the neural connections on the prefrontal cortex, where the hippocampus (learning) and decision-making skills are located, and it increases the neural connections in the amygdala, or the emotion center (remember—fight, flight, freeze or appease). What you see in these students is often a lack of concentration on academics and a heightened emotional state or response state.

Six Hardwired Traits — So What About the Rest?

Every person is born with these six hardwired traits: sadness, joy, disgust, anger, surprise, and fear.[4] These traits can be seen even in the youngest of students. The important thing to understand is that any *other* trait, other than these, needs to be taught. Although traits such as empathy, sympathy, humility, forgiveness, optimism, cooperation and gratitude should be taught at home, if they are not, they must be taught at school.

Hardwired Traits	Learned Traits
Sadness	Humility
Joy	Forgiveness
Disgust	Empathy
Anger	Optimism
Surprise	Compassion
Fear	Sympathy
	Patience
	Shame
	Cooperation
	Gratitude
	Embarrassment
	Drive/determination
	Commitment

I want you to think about your previous five days. Think about different circumstances you encountered where you portrayed the learned traits. How did you respond? Did you show empathy with a neighbor? Gratitude for help? Patience with someone you work with or love? Optimism for a new opportunity? Now I want you to think of how you would have responded if you only had these six traits to work within. Would your reactions have looked differently?

Now think about your classroom or school. What are situations that occur within the four walls of your building where children need to display these learned traits? Let's look at some potential scenarios.

Which hardwired traits would the student possibly demonstrate? How could each student in this scenario respond differently with learned traits?

So many learned responses are taught in this conversation. Does it go the way we want it to 100% of the time when we are teaching these learned responses? Of course not! But we have to start somewhere!

Let's take a look at another possible scenario:

Scenario 1

John has accidentally knocked Tyler's project off the counter and part of it breaks off. If these students have been raised in an environment of poverty, their responses would probably primarily include surprise, anger and fear, and their actions would include running away, passing blame, and name calling. The dialogue could look like this:

Tyler: You're so stupid! Why are you always messing things up? Mrs. Smith, John knocked my project off the counter! He did it on purpose!

John: No, I didn't! I'm not stupid! I didn't do it on purpose!

Here's where we, as teachers, come in. We could react like this:

Mrs. Smith: Both of you, STOP! John, you have to be more careful! When you're running and jumping around, that's going to happen! I told you to all be in your seats!

OR like this:

Mrs. Smith: Oh no, Tyler! I'm so sorry to see that about your project, I know you worked really hard on it (empathy), but I don't think John would knock it off on purpose (optimism). Accidents happen to everyone (empathy)! John, I can see that you feel really sorry for this accident. Can you express that to Tyler (apologetic)?

John: Tyler, I'm sorry I knocked your project over.

Mrs. Smith: Tyler, have you ever accidentally knocked something over? It can happen to anyone, right? I can see that John feels sorry. If you accidentally knocked someone's project off the counter, how would you want that person to respond? Can you respond to John that way (empathy)?

Tyler: It's okay. I just worked really hard on my project.

Mrs. Smith: Great job. Now let's see if maybe during recess we can take a few minutes and work together and see if we can get this project fixed (cooperation).

Scenario 2

Jenny is failing her social studies class because of missed assignments and a failed test. If this student has been raised in poverty, her responses would primarily be anger and fear, and her actions would probably be to give up, quit, and blame the teacher. The dialogue between the student and teacher may look something like this:

Mrs. Taylor: Hi Jenny, I wanted to check in with you on your missing assignments. Would you like to come in after school and work on them?

Jenny: What's the point? You probably won't grade them anyways. You just want to fail me.

Again—here is where our reaction is so crucial. We could respond like this:

Mrs. Taylor: Jenny, I'm not in control of your actions. Only you are. If you cared, you could pass. I can't make you do your work.

OR we could respond like this:

Mrs. Taylor: I'm sorry you feel like that (compassion). I would always give you a fair grade based on the work you did. You seem really frustrated with this class. I know you have a lot going on and a lot you take care of outside of class (empathy). I also know you have great thoughts and ideas (encouragement). What are your goals for this class (determination)? I'd like to see if I can help you get there (cooperation).

Again, notice the learned traits Mrs. Taylor is teaching through modeling.

Where Do We Start?

Now we know many of the causes, and even the effects, of the issues that stem from poverty, but how do we flip this script? This is not a book, or even a chapter, on fixing the issue of poverty. It's on equipping us with the knowledge and tools to facilitate learning and academic success with the students who are faced with these seemingly insurmountable challenges and deficits on a daily basis.

So, let's get started. The first thing we need to realize is that there is a way to meet some of these social and emotional needs, once we know what they are. They include:

- Reliable relationships and social acceptance

- Social skills and conflict resolution/restitution

- Stable, warm environments

- Measurable goals

- Stress reduction techniques[2]

Reliable relationships and social acceptance: Students, specifically in grades fifth through eighth, are highly social beings. This social side actually runs their brains, their feelings, and their behaviors, and those three parts lead to cognition! Their social side directly impacts their ability to learn! This cannot be overlooked, and when this side is lacking, as it often is in students of poverty due to their lack of social skills, their learning is directly impacted. This is such

an important piece to understand. Students need to feel a part of *something*, and if it is not something positive, they will join something negative. Students have this never-ending quest to feel special and unique, without standing out *too much*. Finding this balance is part of the art of being a teacher (bless you, middle school teachers!).

Social skills, conflict resolution and restitution: As we saw in the six hardwired traits, there is much to be taught to growing children, and much to be missed if not taught appropriately. The more we, as educators, can recognize the lack of social skills for what it is and not an act of rebellion or intentional disobedience or disrespect, the more we will be able to fill in the gaps of social skills for these students.

Within social skills, students need to be taught:

- How to ask for help
- How to disagree
- How to meet someone for the first time
- How to help a peer
- How to question authority respectfully
- How to accept "No"

Conflict resolution is one of the most difficult skills for everyone to learn, even adults! This is definitely a skill that must be taught to most students! Restitution falls right in line with this concept. Students must learn how to make things right if they have wronged another person. We saw an example of this in the first scenario earlier in the chapter. Having John help fix the project he accidentally knocked over during recess is an example of restitution—a way for John to help "fix" the problem. Other examples of restitution include writing an apology note, giving back an item that has been taken, or saying something nice about a student that has been made fun of.

Stable, warm environments: When a student finds a stable, warm environment, their affective filter begins to lower, and their brains begin to open back up to learning. Throughout the rest of this book, we will discuss some ways to facilitate this warm, stable environment. Never underestimate the importance of students feeling safe—physically, emotionally and socially—in your class and school. Without this stable environment, you cannot expect learning to take place. This goes directly back to the job of the RAS and the amygdala protecting at all cost.

Measurable goals: Students must create self-efficacy in order to become independent learners, and build the skills needed to be academically successful. Setting measurable goals and then meeting them is one of the best ways to create this self-efficacy. In my research of schools, I have recently come across Aloha-Huber K–8 School in Beaverton, Oregon. This school is a fantastic example of data supporting measurable goal setting. I had the opportunity to speak with the two administrators, and they both emphasized goal setting in two capacities: first, all 1,000 students set social-emotional goals and meet one-on-one with their teacher at least five times during the year. Second, the teachers set goals with common formative assessments,

and then create specific plans for each student who did not master the goals the first time. Their scores and data show the results. For a Title 1 school with 85% poverty, they are scoring above state average in reading and math in all grades, are ranked sixth out of 33 elementary schools in the district, and haven't sent an English learner to high school in 10 years! Goal setting (when paired with accountability) works![5] See the administrators' complete interview in the Teacher Talk section.

Stress-reduction techniques: Learning more response traits immediately expands the student's ability to respond and feel appropriately. Similar to a toddler who throws himself down on the floor of Target when he doesn't get his way, most inappropriate responses are due to an inability to express what the student is actually feeling or needing.

In addition, the heightened level of stress in which the student operates a majority of the time is a constant distractor to learning. Teaching stress-reducing skills can be such a great benefit to students.

When I first started teaching, I taught in a Special Ed classroom. I was the only special education reading teacher for grades six through eight, and I had all disabilities, including emotionally disturbed (which was made up of mostly my students of poverty). I was given a software program to put on my computer in my classroom that was designed to lower the students' stress. For this program, the student would choose a peaceful picture on the screen, and then would put their finger in a monitor, which measured their heart rate. The object of the program was for the student to lower their heart rate. As their heart rate lowered, the picture would begin to go from black and white to color, or the waterfall would begin running, or the hot air balloon

would take off. The students loved this (and there were many times I sat in my room with the lights off and stuck my finger in the heart rate monitor to get the waterfall flowing), but the important skill here was teaching them that they had the power to calm themselves down.

Some common stress reducing activities include:

- Chewing gum

- Teaching your students some yoga moves

- Meditating

- Taking breaks

- Cuddling something—this releases oxytocin, which lowers heart rate and cortisol

- Listening to music

- Laughing

- Tensing and relaxing muscles

- Going for a walk

- Writing your feelings down[5]

The Great Part About The Brain

"A brain that is susceptible to adverse environmental effects is equally susceptible to positive, enriching effects."[2]

It's not hopeless! Though it is challenging, reaching students of poverty is not impossible! Because of the neuroplasticity of our brains, experiences cause region-specific changes to occur, and if those experiences

are positive, positive changes will occur! Brains can change! Thinking can change! Mindsets can change. But it starts with US—changing our mindsets, and the environments and conversations that we have with these students.

> "Brains are designed to reflect the environment they're in, not rise above them. If we want our students to change, we must change ourselves and the environments students spend time in every day."[2]

But What Do We *Do*?

Now we know the causes of the issues, and we know the needs of the students. You're probably getting an idea of what our role as educators is in reaching these students, but let's lay it out clearly here.

We need to:

- Support the whole child—social, emotional, and academic.
- Set high expectations with measurable goals.
- Create a strong, positive environment.
- Model and embody respect.
- Teach social skills and conflict resolution.
- Know when to use positive reinforcement verses punitive punishment.

As we move into the third section of the book, we will continue to look at our roles as teachers with very specific steps for implementation.

Chapter 4 At a Glance

- The brains of students of poverty are often wired differently due to environment, family dynamics, depression, chronic stress, lack of control, and deficits in key developmental skills.

- Students need:

    - Reliable relationships and social acceptance,

    - Social skills and conflict resolution/restitution,

    - Stable, warm environments,

    - Measurable goals, and

    - Stress reduction techniques.

- There are 6 hard-wired traits that all people possess—every other trait must be taught!

- Brains can change!

- We can make a difference if we:

    - Support the whole child—social, emotional, and academic.

    - Set high expectations with measurable goals.

    - Create a strong, positive environment.

    - Model and embody respect.

    - Teach social skills and conflict resolution.

    - Know when to use positive reinforcement verses punitive punishment.

Let's Process

1. What are the learned traits that you use on a daily basis? Where did you learn these?

2. How do you teach and model these traits in your classroom?

3. How do you set measurable goals with your students? How do they measure if they have met these goals? Is there a process put into place?

4. What is the environment in your classroom? What message does it send to the students?

Favorite Resources on This Topic

Why Culture Counts: Teaching Children of Poverty, Sandra Darling and Donna Tileston.[7]

The Learning Brain, Eric Jenson[7]

Teaching with Poverty in Mind, Eric Jenson[2]

Boys in Poverty: A Framework for Understanding Drop-Out, Ruby Payne and Paul Slocumb[8]

PART III
The Implementation

"I've come to a frightening conclusion that I am the decisive element in the classroom. It's my personal approach that creates the climate. It's my daily mood that makes the weather. As a teacher, I possess a tremendous power to make a child's life miserable or joyous. I can be a tool of torture or an instrument of inspiration. I can humiliate or heal. In all situations, it is my response that decides whether a crisis will be escalated or de-escalated and a child humanized or dehumanized."

HAIM GINOTT

*W*e have spent the first two parts of this book looking at the students we have in our classes. We have looked at their backgrounds, cultures, perspectives, and even the reasons for their lack of academic success. Now it's time to dig into the solution!

We are going to break the solution down into four parts:

- Building an alliance
- Creating the environment
- Intentional instruction
- Explicit vocabulary

If we can tackle these areas, we have a really good chance of reaching our students.

So, let's get started!

CHAPTER 5

The Power of an Alliance

"Students work hardest for teachers they like and respect. When I'm asked, 'How do I get the students to like and respect me?' My immediate response is, 'Like and respect them first.'"
— Dr. Debbie Silver

*M*oving students from dependent into independent learners can be a monumental challenge that requires both the teacher and the student working together to increase learning. Many students enter our schools and classrooms with an affective filter that is already high due to previous experiences with teachers or in classrooms. They come in with an "us against them" mentality, automatically looking for reasons to validate that thought. Unfortunately, in many situations, we unintentionally confirm that idea, sometimes without realizing it.

Before we jump into ideas for building an alliance through the lens of being culturally responsive, let's take a look at what an alliance actually demonstrates.

One of the definitions used by dictionary.com for the word

"alliance" is "a merging of efforts or interests by persons, families, states, or organizations."[1] This is the perfect description of what we are talking about when we say we need to form an alliance with our students. They need to know that the teacher and the student are on the same team, working for a common goal. Once this has been established, they can recognize that every task or expectation set before them gets them closer to reaching the common goal.

Intentional Interactions in an Alliance

Now here's the important part—what is the common goal? For the student to pass? Get good grades? Pass the state assessment? Think about the interactions between you and your students. Do your interactions with them sound like this?

"You need to turn work in to bring your grade up."
"You need to come to tutorials to get this work turned in."
"You need to come to tutorials to retake this test."
"You need to get back on task to get this work done. It's for a grade."

Do these statements demonstrate an alliance? Is this teamwork? Does this bring meaning or relevancy to the expectations for the students? What message does this send to the students?

For your middle class, primarily individualist students, grades, passing and getting work turned in will create compliance for them. For the rest of your students, remember, this isn't leverage for them, and they need that alliance.

So let's flip the script.

What if the statements sounded more like these?

"This task will help you understand Andrew Jackson's role in the Civil War, and that's our goal for learning today!"

"It looks like you haven't quite grasped the steps of solving a two-step equation. I want to really make sure you understand this before we move on to inequalities! Can you come spend time with me either after school today or during lunch tomorrow so we can make sure you really understand it! I don't want you to be lost when we move on!"

"You have an important job in this cooperative learning, and not very much time to complete it! Your group won't figure out the hypothesis if everyone isn't on task. Let's refocus! I want you guys to discover the answer!"

"Hey, Nathan. You're missing ___ and ____. Have you done these? We need to make sure you've completed them because that's where we really get to practice making connections within a text. I want you to have the time to practice so you understand all of the connections in the book you picked out. It makes reading so much better when you comprehend it like that. If you need help with this, come see me after school or during lunch!"

What is the difference? Both types of statements redirect students, but the latter statements guide students through a common goal.

The psychology of relationships states that the level of a relationship is based on trust, honesty, respect and communication.[2] Students are looking for these components in a relationship with their teacher as well. When we are talking about our marginalized students, we

have learned that many of them do not have solid relationships outside of the school, nor do they have solid relationships modeled for them. Like every other aspect of culturally responsive teaching that we are discussing, this has to be modeled and taught as well, and it starts with the most influential person in the room—YOU!

Let's shift into *how* we create an alliance. Here are five suggestions:

1. Increase positive, equitable interactions.

2. Have personal conferences for goal setting.

3. Let them see you—how you learn, your goals, how you think.

4. Get to know them on a personal level. Get to know the culture and family.

5. Get rid of the "teacher versus student" mentality.

Equity in Relationships

Students recognize when there is inequity in relationships, and without meaning to, teachers can hurt the alliance with the most needy children. Over 30 years ago, the Los Angeles County Office of Education decided to tackle the problem of inequities in relationships between students and teachers. Using research, they identified 15 interactions that connect to student learning. These are called Teacher Expectations and Student Achievement, or TESA. They contain three main strands, with related interactions:

1. Response Opportunities

    a. Equitable distribution

    b. Individual help

    c. Latency

    d. Delving

    e. Higher-level questioning

2. Feedback

    a. Affirm/correct

    b. Praise

    c. Reasons for praise

    d. Listening

    e. Accepting feelings

3. Personal Regard

    a. Proximity

    b. Courtesy

    c. Personal interest and compliments

    d. Touching

    e. Desist

Interactions within Strands

Response Opportunities	Feedback	Personal Regard
Equitable Distribution: Teacher learns how to provide an opportunity for all students to respond or perform in classroom learning situations.	**Affirm/correct:** The teacher learns how to give feedback to students about their classroom performance.	**Proximity:** The teacher learns the significance of being physically close to students as they work.
Individual help: The teacher learns how to provide individual help to each student.	**Praise for Learning Performance:** The teacher learns how to praise the students' learning performance.	**Courtesy:** The teacher learns how to use expressions of courtesy in interactions with students.
Latency: The teacher learns how to allow the student enough time to think over a question before assisting the student or ending the opportunity to respond.	**Reasons for praise:** The teacher learns how to give useful feedback for the students' learning performance.	**Personal interest and compliments:** The teacher learns how to ask questions, give compliments, or make statements related to a student's personal interest or experiences.
Delving, Rephrasing, Giving Clues: The teacher learns how to provide additional information to help the student respond to a question.	**Listening:** The teacher learns how to apply active listening techniques with students.	**Touching:** The teacher learns how to touch students in a respectful, appropriate, and friendly manner.

Interactions within Strands

Higher-level Questioning: The teacher learns how to ask challenging questions that require students to do more than simply recall information.	Accepting feelings: the teacher learns how to recognize and accept students' feelings in a non-evaluative manner.	Desist: the teacher learns how to stop a student's misbehavior in a calm and courteous manner.[4]

Let's look at the implications of these interactions. Dr. Russell Quaglia, founder of the Quaglia Institute for Student Aspirations, who authored the School Voice suite of surveys, interviewed thousands of students to get their voice on the importance of these interactions. His findings are very interesting, and I think they play in well with culturally responsive teaching.

Let's break the implications of these interactions down by the strands in which they fall.

RESPONSE OPPORTUNITIES

As we look at the collectivist cultures, the value placed on relationships and personal contact can't be overemphasized. The way the students believe the teacher feels about them as a person and as a student becomes a critical indicator of their academic success. Response opportunities are perfect times for students to share their knowledge and ideas. These are also golden opportunities for teachers to show they value their students' voice and ideas. When students are not given an **equitable opportunity** to respond, they look at that lack of a response opportunity as the belief that their teacher doesn't believe in them, or doesn't like them.

Although teachers are aware that the struggling students need more help, students working at grade level or above are often more assertive in asking for help, while those who need the help sit quietly and sometimes invisibly. Also, if we're being transparent, teachers can often gravitate naturally towards helping students with whom they have a stronger relationship.[2]

In order to provide the support necessary for all students to *be able* to respond, a teacher must provide **latency**, or **wait time**. In my opinion, this in one of the easiest ways to immediately affect the level of thinking in your classes, but it has to be intentional. Wait time has several benefits:

- It allows ELs to process the content in their native language or translate if needed.

- It allows students to reread the question (if posted), and process a thought.

- It allows students who have a quick answer to think more critically than an immediate surface answer.

- It gives everyone a chance to think about the question and formulate an answer, even if they are not called on to answer it out loud.

The goal of formulating higher-level questions is to take the students to a deeper level of thinking. As we are intentional about planning and asking higher-level questions, we must provide students time to process and think, and we must be equitable in which students we give the response opportunities!

While having the appropriate amount of wait time can lead to

students building their self-efficacy and autonomy (remember, the brain wants to learn!), not having the appropriate amount of latency can raise the affective filter and build unnecessary frustration, only increasing the learned helplessness.

But let's be honest, wait time can be awkward, especially in upper grades, and especially if this is not part of your practice. Teachers and students alike tend to get restless during time designated only for thinking. I had to be very intentional in my own practice to ensure that I built in wait time.

If using a PowerPoint to project my content and my questions, I would add the words "Wait Time" on the PowerPoint to remind me and to cue the students that this was happening. For me, I had to put some physical movement to it. So when I expect wait time, I point to my brain, say the words, "Nobody talks. Nobody writes. Everybody thinks," and then I walk around the room, counting my steps in my head until I get to the number of seconds I'm allowing for process time.

For example, if I'm giving them 20 seconds of wait time, I will walk around the room, one step per second, until I count to 20 in my head. This accomplishes two things. It provides proximity control and it helps me give them the full 20 seconds they need. You will need to find a way in your own practice that you can build in this wait time.

If you've given the wait time, and the students are still struggling with the question, knowing when and how to delve deeper, rephrase a question, or give clues is imperative for maintaining the positive interactions that build self-efficacy. According to Quaglia, "Teachers tend to ask fewer questions of low-achieving students, interact less frequently with students with whom they have limited

or weak relationships, typically pose easier questions or excuse them from answering if they hesitate, look confused or avert their eyes, and tend to rephrase the question less often, and rarely give students who are less valued clues to be able to answer."[2]

What message does this send? Primarily, the message is that the teacher has little expectation from the student. Humans in general tend to work toward the expectations laid out in front of them, and students are no different. Students will work to the level of expectation given.

Let's circle back to earlier chapters to the development of dependent learners. Asking lower level questions or moving on too quickly to other students does not allow students the opportunity to engage in what neuroscientists call the productive struggle that actually grows brainpower.[4] If our goal is creating independent learners, we must develop the skills of facilitating higher level thinking by asking thought provoking questions, allowing the productive struggle, providing the wait time to think, and giving all students the opportunity to respond.

FEEDBACK

Feedback serves many different purposes. Feedback provides direction for instruction, affirms correct or thoughtful responses, builds self-esteem, and increases value. When students participate in any capacity in class, they want to know what their teachers think about their responses, and students who rely heavily on the relational aspect need it even more. Unfortunately, "lower-achieving students are often ignored or do not receive feedback."[2]

As educators, we must be intentional to ensure that we are acknowledging and affirming all students. We also need to keep in mind that if students are incorrect in their thinking, they typically expect to be corrected. As we are determining the best way and the appropriate times to correct or affirm our students, I think it is always an effective exercise to switch places with the student, thinking through how you would want to be corrected or affirmed. When you throw out an idea or a possible outcome, what response would you like to get? If you are incorrect in an idea, how would you like to be corrected? If you submit a project or write-up to your boss, how would you want to receive feedback? This is a great exercise to help us remember that students, no matter what age, are people as well, and many of the feelings and responses you would have and want are the same for them as well.

While overcorrection can lower self-esteem and self-efficacy, and ultimately lead to poor performance (remember learned helplessness?), the effective teacher learns the balance between affirmation and correction. If all else fails, be intentional and consistent, leaning heavily on the side of affirmation.

Praise is also a very key piece to the positive interactions that promote learning. The Teacher Expectations and Student Achievement document (TESA) suggests that praise should:

- Immediately follow the accomplishment
- Be specific to the accomplishment
- Be informative or appreciative
- Be varied and credible
- Be natural rather than theatrical

- Be individualized
- Be attributed to effort and ability[3]

On Quaglia's Student Voice survey, only 53% of students said that their teachers affirmed them when they tried their best.[2] That means almost half of the students surveyed did not feel praised for their best efforts! When we are reaching the students for whom school is difficult, or where school is their safe place and the teacher is their main role model and leader, not receiving praise in any capacity can be devastating to the student, and detrimental to learning. However, receiving authentic, individualized praise can be just the thing needed to push them over the edge to success and independent learning.

Listening is an important component in the Feedback strand. I love that this is listed as feedback, because giving another person the respect to actively listen sends a very clear message that their voice is valuable. This can be empowering to students who are not used to having their voice heard, or are not confident in sharing their thoughts and ideas. Responding by asking clarifying questions, or agreeing with specific, relevant reasons, making eye contact, and being attentive are all valuable ways to give feedback that the student's voice is valued through the teacher's listening.

To sum up this conversation on feedback, students need to know that you are listening to them, that you value their effort and their voice, and that they are valuable enough to you to offer them feedback.

PERSONAL REGARD

Giving personal regard is a direct response that reveals how you view your students. Personal regard states that you view your students as important people, that you empathize with their thoughts and feelings, and treat them with respect and honor, even if their actions don't necessarily "deserve" it. There will be times when students need to be corrected, redirected, and even disciplined, but all of these interactions still need to be done with a sense of value and respect. Think with me, if you will, about how you expect to be spoken to in local businesses, by your co-workers or administration, and by your family and friends.

Now, reflect for a moment on how you have interacted recently with your most difficult students. Do these match? Interacting in a *courteous*, polite manner sets the culture for how students should interact with each other and you. The ability to *desist*, or correct in a calm and courteous manner, will de-escalate situations and lead to much more learning in your classroom. Unfortunately, in too many classrooms, ethnically and economically diverse students are too often punished with punitive measures (suspension, detention, expulsion, etc.) when many situations could be desisted and de-escalated by the teacher before it reached that point.

Let me take this time to caution you about using sarcasm. Occasionally, you will have students who are able to handle this type of interaction. In a culturally responsive classroom, please be careful with students who may not understand the connotation of the language or have the emotional responses to be able to handle it well.

I remember a technology teacher at one of the high schools where I taught. She had some really creative ideas and projects for the students. However, she offended so many students with her sarcasm that I secretly groaned inside when I saw that my students had her as a teacher. They didn't want to go into her classroom. They certainly

wouldn't go to her for help. That teacher would complain to me that "my kids" would skip her class and didn't turn in work. Everything in me wanted to tell her that she was the problem. I refrained at the time, but I'm not sure I would now. Sarcasm can really hurt the alliance that you are trying to build and stifle learning.

Proximity is such a powerful way to show value and demonstrate a non-verbal interaction that can often redirect with no words. Simply walking near students as you are direct teaching, giving directions, or allowing students to work is a powerful tool for interacting in a non-threatening, positive way. One way I liked to combine proximity and specific praise was to walk around the classroom and put a small check mark on the students' papers who were on task and verbally give them a specific praise. I didn't even acknowledge the students who were choosing to be off task in that moment. Here are some of the phrases they may have heard depending on the task:

"I like the conversation I'm hearing here."
"Thank you for staying in your group."
"Thank you for listening to your partner."
"I like the way you are looking up the answers."
"I like the way I see you using the word wall."
"Thank you for using respectful language with each other."
"Thank you for sharing your thoughts."
"Thank you for writing your thoughts."

My praise was dependent on the learning or behavioral goals I set for the students. If I walked by a student who was not meeting the goals, when I specifically praised the other students around him, that

student almost always quickly followed suit and redirected himself back into the appropriate behavior. Then I was quick to acknowledge this behavior with specific praise.

Another way to increase your positive interactions and build that alliance with the students is to get to know them on a *personal level*. Ask them personal interest questions or give them compliments. Asking specific questions about their family ("Has your mom had her baby yet?") or giving personal compliments ("Hey David, I like your hair cut!") adds an important layer of connection and shows the students that you care about them on more than an academic level. Remember, your students from a collectivist culture will need to know this in order to build that alliance with you, and the alliance leads to learning! The saying, "They don't care what you know until they know that you care" rings very true with students from a collectivist background or students of poverty. Getting to know them on a personal level is a primary way to show that you care, and that you genuinely want to build an alliance.

The last component to mention is *touching*. A personal touch releases endorphins and increases oxytocin, which lowers stress and adds connection. When you can appropriately give a high five, handshake, or hand on the shoulder, it communicates very positive feelings towards the students. Knowing that many of your students of poverty may not receive that personal touch on a regular basis, it makes this type of interaction all the more important and meaningful in creating the alliance.

If praise, affirmation or positive comments are not automatic responses for you, or if you want to be more intentional with these positive interactions with certain students, I recommend the

3:1 method. In this method, you offer three positive praise points for every one correction. At times, this can be a difficult practice. I remember having certain students that I would actually prepare in advance to give praise. As soon as they walked in the door, I was armed with praise. It may have looked something like this:

1. "Good morning, Jose! I'm glad you are here!"

2. "Good job arriving on time!"

3. "How is your mom doing? Has the baby been born, yet?"

This way, when Jose got into my class and was almost immediately off task, I could redirect quickly. He was open to any correction because I had started our interaction off in a positive manner.

Personal conferences for goal setting. There are two really important things that are accomplished when you have a personal conference to set goals. First of all, it gives you the opportunity to connect and have personal contact with each student. Remember that many of these students are walking in with a very negative perception of teachers, and having a one-on-one conversation that gives your total attention to one student, and is positive in nature, is an amazing first step in creating the environment and the alliance needed to propel these students into learning.

Second, you are helping the students set goals. This is also a skill that must be learned. When students self-evaluate where they are currently, and where they need to go, and then you help them put the steps in place needed to meet that goal, an alliance begins. A clear target is formed, and students (and people) become more intrinsically motivated to reach that goal, thus taking another important step towards becoming an independent learner. What an awesome

opportunity, which is so easily overlooked. In teaching, we are constantly making decisions on where to use our time and energy. This is one of those tools, in my opinion, that is worth the time.

Remember Aloha-Huber Park School? Mr. Drue, the Principal, credits individual goal setting, both for academics and social-emotional skills, as one of the top intrinsic motivators for his students, pushing them to move forward by building the self-efficacy they so desperately need in order to be life-long learners!

I want to take a minute and share an excerpt from a blog I wrote on creating an alliance and goal setting with students who are stuck. This blog came from my own personal growth in being a life-long learner.

4 Steps to Influence the Underperformer — and start the move past learned helplessness.
May 27, 2019
From www.pressing-onward.org/blog

Learned helplessness is a very real issue that occurs subconsciously with many of the struggling students, long-term English learners, and students of poverty that struggle year after year. Learned helplessness occurs when students have been conditioned to believe that no matter how hard they work, they cannot move forward. Once they believe that no amount of effort will move them forward, they stop putting forth effort, which ultimately leads to "the shut down." This is such a recurring problem with so many students in so many classrooms.

I'm currently reading *High Performance Habits,* by Brendon Burchard. As I was driving out of town for work this past weekend, I was listening to his podcast #thebrendonshow, and this episode almost jumped out of the speakers at me. Although the book and the podcast are primarily based on business, leadership and personal growth, I couldn't help but make the connection to how we can move the underperformers in our classes to academic success.

One of Brendon's statements that resonated with me was this:

"As a leader, it's your job to let people know when they are not showing up as their best selves. Leaders are forgetting to challenge people to reach their highest level of potential. When leaders coddle, people could underperform their whole lives."[7]

Substitute the word *teachers* for *leaders*, because teachers are the ultimate leaders, and *students* for *people* and this statement makes a whole lot of sense.

As a *teacher*, it's your job to let *students* know when they are not showing up as their best selves. *Teachers* are forgetting to challenge *students* to reach their highest level of potential. When *teachers* coddle, *students* could underperform their whole lives."

This really reached out to me because I know I made this mistake with my students. With only pure motives,

I coddled, helped, and spoon-fed my kids so many times so they could feel "successful," but really, I was just deepening the dependent mentality. I still lose sleep over this sometimes.

This blog is basically my thoughts based on ideas that the awesome podcast put out there. Let's look at four steps to moving the students' mindsets from underperforming to achievement—or from dependent learners to independent learners!

1. Approach students with honor, respect and appreciation.

2. Learn their situation.

3. Challenge how they think.

4. Challenge how they show up.

- **Approach students with honor, respect, and appreciation:** Many of these students feel very little value, and no self-efficacy. Starting a conversation with, "Hey, you're important to me, so I want to have this conversation with you" will go a lot further than, "Why haven't you turned your work in? You're going to fail the class if you don't start working."

- **Learn their situation:** All behavior stems from a reason. Finding out the reason can often help us change the behavior. Asking questions like, "How are you feeling?" and "What are your goals?" and "Do you think you are reaching them?" and then listening to the answers, can give us some real insight as to what's going on. Teachers can't assume why the student is underperforming.

Burchard states, "Never underestimate the potential of God's children. It's the job of the [leader] teacher to stay open to the future potential of their [people] *students*." Wow. It's not for us to judge whether they've got it in them or not—it's just our job to be open to what they could have.

- **Challenge how they think:** "Prompt the students to think differently." Guide students to think about themselves and their contributions differently. Questions like, "Have you thought about it this way?" or "How would your best self handle this situation?" or "What do you think needs to happen in order to take one step forward?" are questions that can challenge the mindset, instead of just focusing on what they haven't done ("Why haven't you turned in that assignment?").

- **Challenge how they show up:** "I know you've got what you need to be successful in this class—can you commit to bring it everyday?" "I'll commit to bringing my best self for you, can you commit to bringing your best self every day to 2nd period?"

I think these steps are great ideas, but I also believe that none of these ideas will work with students unless the teacher has built an *authentic relationship* and *alliance* with the student, with the student fully understanding

that the teacher cares for the student, and that they are on the journey to achievement together. Aren't we held accountable for our students' achievements? Don't we hold ourselves accountable for our students' success? So, in truth, aren't we all trying to reach the same goals?[9]

Let them see you—how you learn, your goals, how you think. Again, you're a team! And you are their role model, and who they get to spend a part of their day with almost every single day. I *in no way* advocate becoming friends with students, oversharing your life, or taking regular time out of instructional time to tell stories. However, they do need to see that you are human, and that you have problem-solving skills and learning goals as well.

Share with them a book that you're reading or something funny that happened over the weekend. If you had an academic struggle that one of your students is having, share how you overcame that. There are definitely appropriate boundaries that need to be set, but there is also a level of humanity that builds an alliance.

Get rid of the "teacher versus student" mentality. We've already touched on this in this chapter, but this is so key. Remember that many students walk in with this mentality, and it's our job to shift their mindset into an alliance mindset. This can be done through all of the steps we are listing here! Be self-reflective throughout the year. Does your classroom shift into this "teacher verses student" mentality throughout the year?

Think back to the scenarios in outlined in chapter 1 of the

book—the friend crying in the bathroom, the sick grandmother in Mexico, the student already working a full time job. The way we handle situations like these will be one of the deciding factors on if we can build an alliance with the student, even across cultures. Or will we send the message that our culture and perspective is right and theirs is wrong? If we do, the "teacher verses student" line is drawn and we were the ones who drew it.

We also have to consider that many students walk into the school or classroom with this mentality already engrained in their minds. Perhaps they have had a teacher in the past who did not form an alliance. Perhaps their parents had a bad experience in school and have passed that thinking along. We may have to break through this thinking and intentionally build the alliance.

Remember, your students from an individualistc culture, with parents who put an emphasis on education and good grades, may not need this alliance, but the rest of your precious students will. If our job is to facilitate learning, and they need this alliance to learn, we need to build it!

Chapter 5 At a Glance:

Building an alliance is key to promoting learning in the classroom. Four ways to do this are

- Personal conferences for goal setting.

- Let them see you—how you learn, your goals, how you think.

- Get to know them on a personal level. Get to know the culture and family.

- Get rid of the "teacher versus student" mentality.

Let's Process

1. What are common phrases you hear yourself say to students? Do these phrases create an alliance or a "teacher verses student" mentality?

2. Think of some of your students who may be struggling in your class. How do you think *they* view your role and relationship? Would they say you are in an alliance with them?

Strategies for Implementation

Strategies for building an alliance with the student:

- Set common goals.

- Celebrate learning victories.

- Be intentional with the verbiage used to redirect—put the focus on learning and not on completion or a grade.

Strategies to build an alliance with the parents and families:

- Build a positive relationship without expectations before asking the parent to take action on something.

- Give specific points of praise about their student.

- Value their voice and expertise on their student.

Favorite Resources on This Topic

Engagement by Design, Fisher, Frey and Quaglia[2]

Culturally Responsive Teaching and the Brain, Zaretta Hammond[4]

High Performance Habits, Brendon Burchard[8]

CHAPTER 6

The Beauty of a Culturally Rich Environment

"Brains are designed to reflect the environments they're in,
not rise above them. If we want our students to change,
we must change ourselves and the environments
students spend time in every day."[1]
— Eric Jenson

*a*s we continue on our journey to becoming a culturally responsive teacher, we have to take a deeper look at creating an
environment conducive to learning for all students. We are going to
look at this in two different sections:

- Setting clear expectations with processes and procedures
- Facilitating a collaborative climate through cooperative
  learning

Setting Clear Expectations with Processes and Procedures

The first point made above directly links to lowering the affective filter. We have to remember that many of the students we are working with live and deal with a great amount of chaos in their daily lives. Setting clear expectations, and having processes and procedures in place, creates a sense of stability and structure. Let's dive in.

Having clear expectations in your classroom gives students a direct target to hit. When working with this group of students, fairness is one of the key characteristics that many look for in a teacher. Most students will accept responsibility; they just don't want to be singled out. When a teacher doesn't have clear expectations, and students don't know exactly where the target is, the class expectation becomes much more subjective and emotionally driven. This is when teachers often behave more *reactively* instead of *proactively*.

For example, do students need to raise their hand before they speak? Is this true for all students, 100% of the time?

When can students go to the bathroom? Is this clear for all students? Are you firm on these times?

Can students talk to each other during work time?

We counter the frustration that is caused by moving expectations by being proactive—by setting clear expectations, reminding students of the clear expectations, and directing them back to the expectations when they need to be redirected.

Questions:

1. If I don't acknowledge one student's answer because he didn't raise his hand, but then 15 minutes later, I listen

to another student who calls out, what message am I sending? Do I even recognize I'm doing this?

2. If one student asks to go to the restroom and I say "no," and then five minutes later, another student asks to go to the restroom and I say "yes," what message does this send?

3. If two girls are talking in the back of the room while they are working and I tell them to stop talking, and then two students start talking in another part of the room and I don't say anything, what message am I sending?

4. Do I have clear expectations laid out, or am I responding to students in a reactionary manner?

Being inconsistent, and what students perceive as "unfair," even if completely unintentionally, is one of the best ways to raise the affective filter, damage the alliance, and shut the door to learning. We are all human, and it is never possible to respond 100% equally to all students; hence, the need for procedures that take the guesswork out.

The system of CHAMPS[2] is a model that I highly recommend for teaching and setting expectations. It most likely won't take care of every behavior issue, but it will help the teacher intentionally think through the processes and procedures that are important to him or her in different situations in the classroom.

Even if you don't use a premade system like CHAMPS, the central idea is that both the teacher and the student are aware of the expectations. What do the students do if they need help? Have a question? Have an answer? Need to sharpen their pencil or go to the restroom? What does independent work like? Cooperative learning? Partner work?

The list can go on, but the importance is thinking through your expectations for these situations and teaching those expectations clearly. Nothing can be assumed. Teach everything! For students of poverty or culturally diverse students, they may have been raised with different "norms" in the home than you were. You can't expect them to fall into your norms if they haven't been taught and had the time to practice. Remember, we all have a cultural lens in which we are viewing the world. *As teachers, it is never our job to judge, critique or change different cultures, only to promote learning. If we have expectations that are set from our cultural lens, we have to be clear about those, and model in a way that is respectful, with student learning as the clear target.*

As an example, I remember when I first started working at a high school, which at the time was predominantly an African American school. I was amazed at how much the students yelled greetings to one another! Most of it was positive, with laughing and high fives and handshakes, but to my dismay, they were literally yelling down the hallway and in my classroom. I came from a small, generally quiet family, and the idea of yelling out in a public place wouldn't have even been thought of, much less encouraged. We weren't even allowed to yell at each other from another room in the house.

One day, I was standing in the immense hallway of this school, and a parent of one of my students walked into the building, saw one of her daughter's friends down the hallway, and yelled out *"HEY MISHA! HOW ARE YOU DOING? TELL YOUR MAMA 'HI' FOR ME!"*

Well, there you go. I'm not going to change the nature of communication, nor do I want to, but I can teach my expectations of voice levels when you enter my classroom so that we can begin learning quickly. Will my students need to practice this? Sure! Will they get it in the first week? Some won't. But I can almost guarantee that they will by the first month—if I am consistent.

In my interview with the administrators of Aloha-Huber Park School, Vice Principal, Mr. Alfonso Giardiello, emphatically stated, "The pathway to student independence has to be modeled. Teachers must be clear on the steps. They cannot assume the students know. It's an intentional process." How true.

It's also important to remember that while students may not verbally express that they love the structured classroom, the safety and security that a structured classroom brings is exactly what these struggling students need in order to function at their highest level. So, while you may not want to be the overly structured teacher, if you want to be culturally responsive, a big piece of that is creating a safe and inviting environment. Having clear expectations, with processes and procedures put into place, creates that effective classroom system.

I was working with a brand new teacher who had taken over a very challenging seventh grade math class halfway through the year. She did not have appropriate processes or procedures, and she had a very high-needs class. I had been in that class a few times, and I just couldn't take it anymore. I finally (abrubtly) got the students' attention and asked these questions:

"How many of you want to learn in this class?" All but two students raised their hands.

"How many of you want a good grade in this class?" All but two students raised their hands.

"How many of you want to pass the state exam you're about to take in a few weeks?" All but two students raised their hands.

"How many of you are tired of a few students keeping the rest of you from learning?" All but two students raised their hands. Now the two started feeling uncomfortable.

"How many of you are ready to ignore inappropriate behavior, respect your teacher, help each other out, and let her teach?" All but two students raised their hands. But, the class was perfect the rest of the day.

I only tell you this to say, that even in the most chaotic class, most students want to learn. Most students want to do what is right. Remember that their social brain runs their actions, so they succumb to peer pressure more than we would like. Students want to feel successful, but chaos breeds more chaos. Giving them the skills and the expectations that they need sets them up for the success we all want.

STUDENT-CENTERED CLASSROOMS

Along with setting clear expectations, setting up a student-centered classroom, where students have ownership of the culture, climate and learning, is a fantastic way to build an environment set up for culturally responsive teaching.

I repeatedly hear administrators state the importance of a "self-run" classroom taking care of most behavior issues and promoting learning almost more than any other singular factor. As we are trying to promote independent learners in our classroom, we have to be willing to let go of some of the control and let the students take ownership of the class. Do a quick check. Where does your classroom style fall?

Teacher Centered Classroom	Student Centered Classroom
Lecture based	Hands on
Majority whole group instruction	Academic dialogue is occurring among students
Teacher gives all verbal directions	There is choice in learning tasks
Teacher voice is more prevalent than student voice	Students know where to find directions or get help apart from the teacher
Teacher asks majority of questions	
Classroom is typically quiet	

FACILITATING COOPERATIVE LEARNING

We know that students from the collectivist culture innately rely on, help and trust each other. They work together, live together, and take care of each other. It is only expected that they would *naturally* learn better working cooperatively. Before we consider some of the hurdles to overcome when implementing cooperative learning, let's look at what cooperative learning is and why it is so important.

WHY COOPERATIVE LEARNING?

In *Productive Group Work*, Fisher, Frey and Everlove, state that in cooperative learning, "students end up educating one another and end up knowing **more than they would have working alone**."[3] (*Emphasis added.*) I believe this statement is one of the most crucial benefits to facilitating successful cooperative learning. In the many classrooms I have had the opportunity to visit, I see students working

on independent work with the option of talking to their group. Not surprisingly, the result is that most of the students are off task, chatting about anything other than the assignment, and the teacher is constantly redirecting conversations and frustrated at their output. More importantly, how much learning is actually taking place? If we look at the statement above, they should be educating each other and learning *more* than if they were working alone.

As teachers, we have to be aware of this. If we have given a task, and the students are not learning more together than they would on their own, we need to either restructure the cooperative learning tasks, or that particular task needs to be independent work. Otherwise, it just takes away from the learning, and the learning task becomes counterproductive.

HOW TO MAKE IT SUCCESSFUL

"We must view group work as more than a means of completing a project or task. Productive group work is an essential stepping stone to learning and mastery."[3]

How do we move cooperative learning from off-task conversations to meaningful learning? Let's take a look at four steps to help your students achieve success in cooperative learning groups:

1. Set, model and teach clear processes, procedures and expectations.
2. Set the goals for learning, not completion.

3. Plan the logistics based on the task and your students.

4. Affirm voice and thought.

Let's dig in a little deeper.

1. **Set, model and teach clear processes, procedures and expectations**, as discussed at the beginning of this chapter. What voice level should the students be on, and have they practiced this? What should their conversations sound like? What do they do if they need help? Are they allowed to get out of their seats? By proactively reminding students of this at the beginning, it will cut down on the number of reactionary comments you have to make. Don't assume anything!

2. **Set the goals for learning, not completion**. Think about the difference in these two statements:

   a. "Class, work together as a group to read the excerpt and complete the chart on conflict."

   b. "Class, work together as a group to read the excerpt and figure out how the different conflicts in this story affect the plot. You'll need to be able to identify three different conflicts and explain to me how they affected the plot. You can use the chart on the table to help you gather your thoughts. Each of your roles are defined in the directions on the table, but all of you will need to be able to explain how conflict affects the plot, so help each other understand!"

How will the output be different in these cases? Same groups. Same assignment. Different focus for learning.

In the first statement, I can almost guarantee that in mixed-ability groups, one person will carry the majority of the load, reading the excerpt and filling out the chart. Then, the rest of the group will copy. They will turn in the chart, score a 100% or close to it, and three out of the four students still won't be able to answer a question about how conflict affects plot because they haven't done any thinking or learning. See the problem here?

In the second statement, although they still have a chart to complete, the chart is a resource to help them with the learning. They have a goal for learning, and the expectation that everyone can explain their learning, not simply turn in the chart. Also, the teacher has clearly defined roles for each person in the group, which could include reading separate paragraphs, looking for specific ideas within the text, proving answers within the text, or filling out the chart with the explanations from the others.

Our students trick us at times. We are explaining the directions, and inevitably, a hand shoots up with the question, "Is this for a grade?" That makes us, the teachers, think that students must have a grade to find value in the work. The truth is that they have been conditioned to think that a grade equals importance on an assignment. This is because our conversations with them often center on missing papers, retaking tests they failed, and passing a class. But, remember, the brain wants to learn! If you think about that situation, most of the time, when a student asks that question, it's not so that he strives to make a 100 and do his best. It's that he either copies or makes a 70, because passing is his only goal when it comes to grades. However,

how awesome would it be if, going back to the second example above, when the student asked, "Is this for a grade?" our response was:

> "I haven't decided yet. You need to learn how the conflict is a really important part of the story, and impacts so much of the events in the story. And to see that when you write a story, a good conflict can make or break your story! I will look at your charts to see your ideas, but I'm also listening to your conversations and your explanations. If I take a grade, it will take all of those things into consideration."

As opposed to:

> "Yes. You will turn the charts in at the end of class."

This is so powerful, and a good shift in focus for all areas of your instruction, not just cooperative learning. Remember that we are building independent learners—problem solvers and risk takers who put in the effort to learn, but grades will not motivate learning.

Do grades motivate some kids? Absolutely. Students from the individualist culture will more than likely be all about grades, but focusing on the learning will only increase their success as well. The grades will follow.

3. **Plan the logistics based on the task and your students**. Sometimes, there are simple fixes within a classroom to help with cooperative learning.

    a. You, the teacher, create the groups. Whether you are doing it for behavior reasons, ability grouping, or language proficiencies, when you create the groups, you have more control over who is working with whom. You also send a message that says, *"This is intentional work time"* and not, *"This is hang out and visit with your friends time."* Eventually, after your students have shown that they can have productive cooperative learning groups for an ongoing period of time, perhaps they can group themselves, but not before.

b. Think about time. The average middle school student has an eight-minute attention span on one activity, unless it is *super*-intriguing. To have students work together on one task for 25 minutes is really setting an unreasonable expectation for most students. Chunk the assignment, especially for classes that need a higher structure. Set a timer.

"Group, you have eight minutes to read the excerpt. Person assigned to read paragraph 1, give me a thumbs-up when you are ready to go. Ok, I see everyone's thumbs. You may begin!"

This gets them started immediately, and creates a sense of urgency to stay on task. They also only have to process one step of the task at a time. Again, as they practice and master the art of working cooperatively, you can back off on the need for such a high structure.

c. Create intentional proximity control. This is not the time to be behind a desk, even though the students are working with each other. For high structure classes, which students of poverty, LTELs, and culturally and ethnically diverse students typically create, they need your presence. Oftentimes, I would use this time to walk around and give checkmarks or stickers for being on task, having the conversations I've laid out for them to have, or affirming their thinking or ideas. This is a very positive way to redirect off-task behavior as well.

d. Make sure the directions are posted. As soon as students don't know what to do next, off-task behavior begins!

4. **Affirm voice and thought.** If you have set the expectation of academic dialogue and learning, it is important to affirm those specific expectations. Think about these two statements:

a. "I really like the conversations you guys are having. You're doing a great job of proving your answer. Jose, do you agree with your group? Why is that? I like that thought! Make sure you get it written down. Group, write Jose's idea down. It was a good one."

b. "Jose, you don't have anything on your chart filled out. Get back on task! You only have 10 minutes left in class."

Let's think about what each statement has done. In the first statement, the teacher has redirected Jose back into participating with the group by asking his opinion and then asking him to explain. The teacher then validates his ideas by reminding the group to write down what Jose said. This affirms and validates Jose's thoughts and voice, and it redirects him back into the group.

In the second statement, the focus is on the chart. With time dwindling, Jose will most likely copy the other group members' charts (if he cares about the teacher and wants to turn something in for him), but will likely have no input or learning occurring at all.

The way we approach these students and their learning is so crucial to moving them into independent learners.

SOME OF THE ISSUES WITH COOPERATIVE LEARNING

Here's the problem: Many students, especially those who are culturally, linguistically and economically diverse, *don't know how* to work together academically. We've already mentioned that many of these students are coming in with vocabulary deficits and communication differences.

How do we counteract this? We teach them!

Sentence frames are incredibly powerful for creating academic dialogue and building the vocabulary needed to have these types of conversations.

There are two types of sentence frames I would recommend. One type is called academic sentence frames. One great resource for this is *DOK Question Stems and Response Frames,* from EL Saber Enterprises. These help the student with the language of the dialogue needed to discuss the content. See the examples in Exhibit 2:

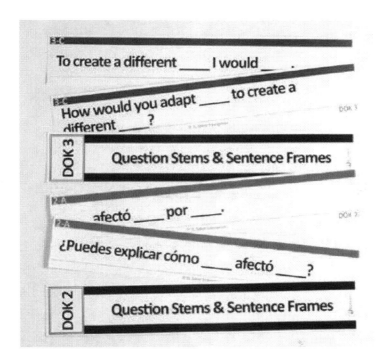

To create a different _____ I would _____.

How would you adapt _____ to create a different _____?

DOK 3

Question Stems & Sentence Frames

_____ afectó _____ por _____.

¿Puedes explicar cómo _____ afectó _____?

DOK 2

Question Stems & Sentence Frames

Another type of sentence frames is called accountable talk frames. These have the language to help students communicate with each other in a respectful manner while sharing their ideas at the same time.

To illustrate the power of these frames, I want to include a blog that I wrote on this topic after working with a group of middle school teachers in the Bronx, NY. I had nothing to do with getting these conversations started, but I sure got to see the benefit of them happening!

Teaching By Reaching On The Power Of Conversation – From Dominican Middle Schoolers In The Bronx

JANUARY 29, 2019

From www.pressing-onward.org/blog

"My kids won't stay on topic."

"My students can't control themselves."

"My students won't participate."

"My students won't interact with kids they don't like."

Is it worth it to push through all of these "problems" and facilitate conversations?

YES!

We all have pet peeves, and one of mine is the phrase, "My students can't do that." UGH! It literally takes everything I can do not to yell, "NO, FRIEND (that's my nice version). It's YOU."

I have had the pleasure of working through EL Saber Enterprises at I.S. 232 Middle School in the Bronx, NY. (Cardi B's middle school, for those who care :).) We are working primarily with the ESL and bilingual kids at this middle school.

One of the beautiful initiatives that Mrs. Resto, the Principal, has put into place is accountable talk.

So I want you to get the full picture here:

A classroom full of students from the Dominican Republic who have been in the country less than three years, with teachers teaching grade level material in English, but able to clarify in Spanish if needed, an intentional push for higher level, rigorous questions to be asked in the classroom, a neighborhood set in generational poverty.

The question is posed: How has learning about the role of a salesman influenced how you feel about Willie in *The Death of a Salesman?*

Teacher: Think about this question. (Wait 10 seconds.) Now turn to your shoulder partner and discuss your answer and respond to your partner. Person with the longest hair goes first. (Students discuss – some in English and some in Spanish, but all talking about the question.)

Teacher: Who would like to share? (Students almost come out of their seats trying to answer the question.) Jose?

Jose: Learning about the role of a salesman makes me understand why Willie is so negative, so I feel more sorry for him.

Teacher: Oh, I like that you have a feeling towards him. Who can add to that? Ana?

Ana: I agree with what Jose said, but I will also add that I think Willie works really hard and is told no a lot.

Teacher: Good observation, Ana, but how does that make you feel about Willie?

Ana: I feel like I understand why Willie is rude because I don't like someone to tell me no.

Teacher: Excellent job being empathetic! You are understanding how Willie feels! Who would like to add to that? Manuel?

Manuel: I like what Ana said, but I agree with Jose that I feel sorry for Willie. I feel sorry because he has so much pressure.

Y'ALL! THIS HAPPENED WITH SIXTH GRADERS!

I was blown away. These students were listening and responding, thinking deeply about the content, and forming their own opinions – and it all started with conversation.

So I got to thinking about the importance of conversation. To answer my question posed above, **YES! IT IS ABSOLUTELY** worth the time and effort it takes to have these conversations. But if middle school

students (God bless them) from another country in a high poverty area can use accountable talk to have academic conversations, then there is no reason to say that anyone can't do it.

We just have to teach them.

Briefly, here's four ways:

- Use sentence frames. Teach them the words to use and when to use them.

- Model. Model. Because the teacher modeled the conversation, and then used the accountable talk stems in whole group, the students learned how to use those stems in small groups – and we saw this in EVERY CLASS.

- Value their voice. This theme keeps coming up, but if the students don't feel that their thoughts and opinions are important, they have no reason to speak them. Applaud those who are brave enough to share their voice. Every time. Facilitate the class's applause. Kids need to learn how to value others as well.

- Don't be afraid to ask questions that require the students to **a)** think, and **b)** process through with their partner or group. If we ask easy questions, the students don't have anything to discuss![4]

This was such an amazing example of how conversation promoted learning, and how students *can be taught* to have these types of conversations! It's just our job to do it!

Fisher and Frey explain Johnson and Johnson's five principles for making the right conditions for productive group work:

1.   Positive interdependence

2.   Face-to-face interaction

3.   Individual and group accountability

4.   Interpersonal and small group skills

5.   Group processing

Positive Interdependence

If you think about working together in a small group as an adult, whether in Positive Learning Communities (PLC), an action team on the board of a committee, or planning a party for a friend's birthday, you probably don't all work on one task, then all go to the next task, and so forth. More than likely, you each have a role and a deadline, and probably even an outcome for which you are responsible and receive credit. You're probably not going to all go to the grocery store to get food, then all stand in the kitchen and cook the same dish, then all go get the decorations, then all decorate in the same room. That would not be an effective or efficient way to work together.

This is also true in an academic setting. Positive interdependence occurs when each member of the group needs the other members to contribute in order to effectively meet the challenge presented.

Johnson and Johnson list four suggestions to consider when creating positive interdependence in a group:

1. Goals

2. Resources

3. Rewards

4. Roles

Remember that all of these don't have to be implemented every time, but they are all great ways to create the positive interdependence we're looking for.

Goals. We know that setting meaningful and measurable goals gives us a target to hit, and with a target to hit, we are more likely to get it done. In positive interdependence, each member of the group has a goal to hit, and when these goals are met, the overall goal of the group can be met.

In our example under *Set the Goals for Learning*, this is how the activity could possibly play out:

Member A: Goal: Finish reading the excerpt out loud in 10 minutes, ensure that each person in the group can explain how the conflict impacts the events in the plot, and check the chart to make sure it is filled out.

Member B: Identify the internal conflict within the main character.

Member C: Identify the external conflict between the two characters in the excerpt.

Member D: Identify events in the plot that were affected by the conflicts.

Goal as the group: Write and explain how both conflicts impacted the events in the excerpt.

Each person has a specific goal to achieve in order to meet the group goal. This gives each person an important learning task, and facilitates the participation of each member.

Resources. Distribute resources so that each person in the group has a unique piece of information. For example, if the group is answering questions, give each person a separate question. This takes away the opportunity for one person to do the whole assignment, and requires the members to work with each other. In the example above, the excerpt could be chunked:

Member A: Has the entire excerpt and the chart.

Member B: Only has the section containing the internal conflict and a place to document findings.

Member C: Only has the section containing the external conflict and a place to document findings.

Member D: Has the entire excerpt and perhaps a flow map to document the events directly affected by the conflicts.

Rewards. Rewards are given for individual and group efforts. This pulls in the individualistic and collectivist cultures, but it doesn't have to necessarily mean just grades. This could be affirmations, extra time on technology, being chosen as a model group, or getting to choose when they share their findings.

Roles. Each member's separate job is necessary to completing the task. This goes hand-in-hand with setting individual goals to meet the common goal. This is a great litmus test for you, the teacher, to know whether or not you have set up a situation where cooperative learning is necessary.

Face-to-Face

With the new age of technology, face-to-face interactions are becoming more obsolete. Our students don't even have face-to-face conversations and interactions in social situations anymore, making it all the more difficult to have face-to-face interactions in an academic setting. This is a real struggle that we have to overcome.

When we are encouraging face-to-face interactions, these should be "designed to encourage the exchange of ideas and not just to work out the logistics of completing the assignments."[3] They need to talk to each other about the content, and about their *opinions* on the content. One great way to do this is to design questions and academic dialogue that requires students to discuss it in this way.

Sample questions to discuss:

1. What is the internal conflict with the main character? "Member B, share your answer."

2. "Member A, do you agree or disagree with this answer? Explain your answer."

3. "Member C, have you ever had an internal conflict similar to this one? Explain if you have, and if not, explain how you would handle it if you did have that conflict."

4. "Member D, if you were the main character, would you have handled it the same way he did? If not, how would you have handled it differently?"

5. "Member A, if this internal conflict were handled differently, how would the events in the plot change?"

6. "Group, you have two minutes to discuss any last minute thoughts on this topic."

Question stems are also a fantastic resource to use to help with face-to-face interactions.

Individual and Group Accountability

Students and adults alike need feedback. We need to know that what we are doing matters and is meeting expectations. It is important to hold both the individual and group accountable. It's key to note here that I'm not simply referring to grades. Oftentimes, saying, "You are working in a group, but you're going to earn your individual grade" actually kills the cooperative learning. If I think that another member

of the group has an idea that will bring my grade down, why would I be open to listening to his ideas? There are so many other ways to hold students accountable:

- **Specific praise:** This is not just saying, "You guys are doing a good job!" Praising the specific skill you are trying to build may sound like "I really like the way your group is discussing the different ideas you all are bringing to the table. You are disagreeing and defending your points with text evidence! Way to go!"

- **Individual praise within the group context:** "Madison, I really like the way you agreed with Jose and then added your own thought!"

Interpersonal and Small-Group Skills

This is possibly the most important and basic set of skills to teach if you want your students to be able to have the conversational skills that lead them to higher level thinking. This includes asking and receiving help, accountable talk (agreeing and disagreeing well), eye contact, listening skills, and taking turns. Students must learn to share the load and carry their own weight.

Think about the last time you sat down with a group of adults to accomplish a task. What interpersonal skills did the group possess? Were there any that were lacking? What was the result? If you were in a group that had a good set of interpersonal skills, chances are you made headway on your task and it was a fairly enjoyable experience. If, however, people in the group lacked interpersonal skills, there may have been arguing, people trying to take over the group, people

disconnected from the group, and overall a lack of progression in the task or project.

So why do we expect our students to automatically have these skills? These skills need to be taught, modeled, practiced, and practiced some more!

Group Processing

"The opportunity for groups to talk to one another about what worked and what didn't is crucial to future success."[3]

Students need a voice in the processes. They need to hold themselves, and their groups, accountable, as well as gather ideas from other groups. This is how they build their problem-solving skills, interpersonal skills, and face-to-face skills. Leaving five minutes at the end of an instructional period for groups to process with each other will set up future cooperative learning opportunities for success. When students claim that "this worked" or "that didn't work," moving forward, students can share the ownership in facilitating the cooperative learning for their own success. For example, if students say that they like the directions being on the desk, having technology as a reference, and sentence frames to help with the conversations, then those tools can be used again, and the students begin to evaluate what works for them! This is a great tool in building autonomy.

Here are the important take-aways of cooperative learning.

For many of your students, this is the number one way to increase their learning and build language. Cooperative learning must be intentional and planned, and the students must need the other group members in order to meet the challenge or complete the task if cooperative learning is going to be successful. And lastly, teachers must teach, model and practice the skills necessary for students to successfully learn in cooperative learning groups.

Chapter 6 At a Glance

To have a culturally responsive environment conducive to learning, you must have clear expectations with processes and procedures, and the students must have productive cooperative learning opportunities.

Four steps to help your students achieve success in cooperative learning groups:

1. Set, model and teach clear processes, procedures and expectations.

2. Set the goals for learning, not completing a task.

3. Plan the logistics based on the task and your students.

4. Affirm voice and thought.

Don't assume that students know the appropriate way to interact and learn in cooperative learning groups. Model and teach everything!

Let's Process

1. How do you communicate your expectations to your students?

2. What are your processes and procedures that help create that safe, structured environment?

3. What does cooperative learning look like in your classroom?

Strategies for Implementation

Strategies for facilitating cooperative learning groups:

1. Model and practice appropriate voice levels and academic conversations.

2. Provide sentence frames to build language and facilitate appropriate academic dialogues.

3. Make sure every member of the group is needed.

4. Give group and individual accountability and affirmation (apart from grades).

Favorite Resources on This Topic

Kagan Cooperative Learning, Dr. Spencer Kagan[5]

Stra-tiques, EL Saber Enterprises[6]

ELPS at a Glance, EL Saber Enterprises[7]

CHAPTER 7

The Effectiveness of Hitting the Learning Target

"If a child can't learn the way we teach, maybe
we should teach the way they learn."

— Ignacio Estrada

*N*ow that we have built up a positive alliance with our students and setup our environment for structure and collaboration, we are ready to address the learning and instruction.

I was talking to a principal the other day about culturally responsive teaching. As we discussed the fact that simply building a relationship was not enough to ensure academic success, she stated emphatically, "Thank you for saying that!" She went on to say, "If one more person tells my teachers to just build a relationship, someone's going to lose it!" The relationship is key to opening students up to learning, but we have to be intentional about the instruction as well.

What does this look like? Let's break it down into five different parts:

1. Clear learning targets

2. Feedback and formative assessment

3. Aligned and meaningful tasks

4. Differentiation

5. Vocabulary

Clear Learning Targets

We cannot underestimate the importance of setting clear learning targets. Although this seems to be common knowledge, I am constantly amazed by how many teachers are either unclear as to the learning target or have completion of a task as the learning target.

If you haven't picked up on the focus of culturally responsive teaching, *learning* definitely takes precedence over *doing*. The doing should always facilitate and connect to the learning, giving relevance to the task, and keeping the students focused on learning, because that is where autonomy and intrinsic motivation set in.

Look at the difference in these statements:

1. Students will complete worksheet on Pg. 7–8.

2. Students will understand how to setup and solve two-step equations from word problems.

Which one is a learning target?

So where do teachers get their learning targets? Each state is given a set of standards, and the learning targets should come directly from these standards. In fact, the learning target could be the standard. One helpful suggestion for determining the exact learning the state requires is to deconstruct each standard. This is the process of simply

determining what students must *know* and *do* in order to master the standard. Let's take a look at this standard as an example:

Analyze how dialogue between characters contributes to the conflict resolution.

I could break this down into what students need to know and do like this:

Know	Do
Dialogue	Identify dialogue
Characters	Identify conflict resolution
Conflict	Analyze how dialogue contributes to conflict resolution
Conflict resolution	

Oftentimes, the standard is not meant to be learned in one day, or standards are bundled together. This is where you should start. Understand the end goal of these standards. Decide how many days it will take to teach the standard, and then determine a learning goal for each day of the lesson.

For example, let's look at a sample plan.

Standard: Analyze how dialogue between characters contributes to the conflict resolution.

You may determine that it will take four days for students to master this standard. You break the instruction into four days and determine a learning goal for each day that builds to mastery of this standard.

Day 1: Students will define, identify, and state the importance of dialogue in the text.

Day 2: Students will find and identify conflict resolution in the text.

Day 3: Students will analyze how dialogue between characters contributes to the conflict resolution in a group.

Day 4: Students will analyze how dialogue between characters contributes to the conflict resolution independently.

Another value of setting clear learning targets is having the expectation for learning. In a study done by Russ Qualia on 48,185 students, 27% of them reported that they don't think their teachers expect them to be successful (p 25).[1] That's almost three out of ten. Unfortunately, this percentage is going to lean heavily towards the students we are representing in this book; the students who need this expectation more than anyone else.

Interestingly enough, in a study by John Hattie, teacher clarity was the most impactful contribution to student learning.[1] Clarity asks these basic questions:

1. What are you learning?
2. Why are you learning it?
3. How will you know when you learned it?

Both teacher and student should be able to answer these questions every day. When everyone is clear on the learning, this adds value to

the alliance between teacher and student, gives the teacher a target to assess, and gives the student a goal to reach. All of these factors play an immense role in student learning and achievement.[1]

I've seen some of the most creative activities out there, but if they are not directly leading to learning, are we doing our job as educators, or are we simply entertaining? I've witnessed projects that last a week with no real learning taken place. I've observed walls decorated with beautiful art that created no real learning. I've watched days of stations where the students are just *doing*, with no connection to *learning*.

Feedback and Formative Assessment

"Feedback is the effort to close the gap between current performance and desired outcomes. But feedback is far less effective when students are not clear on what those desired outcomes are."[1]

Once there is a clear learning target, it is imperative to measure students' mastery of the learning along the way. For our struggling students, if we are not constantly, formatively assessing their learning, they could go several days with lost learning. If we are focused on the product or if we don't have daily learning targets, we can lose sight of what we are supposed to teach.

Look at these questions:

1. Did we complete our worksheet pages?

2. Solve this problem: Ben is an aspiring music artist. He

has a record contract that pays him a base rate of $200 a month and an additional $12 for each album that sells. Last month he earned a total of $644. Write an equation to determine the number of albums Ben sold.

Which question helps the students and the teachers evaluate their learning for the day?

Formative assessment does not have to be a grade, or formal, or a quiz, or in any specific format. Formative assessment is a way to give ongoing feedback and to make the student and teacher aware of how close the student is to mastering the goal.

When you are planning formative assessment, please keep the following in mind:

1. Formative assessment should be done individually. If you are using cooperative learning as a formative assessment to determine where the students are in their learning, you may find you are only assessing the strongest member of the group.

2. Formative assessment should eventually be without resources or notes. If the expectation is that the student can classify compounds and mixtures without notes, and you are letting the student use his notes, you are really assessing his notetaking, not his learning.

3. Formative assessment should be aligned to the learning target. Asking a question like, "What was the most surprising thing about the text we read today?" is a great debrief question, but is not aligned to a learning target, and therefore doesn't measure a skill.

4. Formative assessment must be useful to the teacher. If you are a secondary teacher and you have 150 students, trying to grade 150 papers every night to give immediate feedback is not feasible. Make it easy on yourself! I strongly recommend technology for formative assessments. Programs like *Plickers*[2] are fantastic ways to allow technology to quickly gather data and make the feedback useful. If the formative assessments aren't used to drive your instruction, they are really a waste of time and resources for everyone involved!

Aligned and Meaningful Tasks

I often hear: "My students won't turn their work in." "My student won't come to tutorials." "My students won't stay on task." "My students will only work if it's for a grade."

The primary issue here may be that students are not finding relevance in the tasks or cooperative learning. When we can build tasks that directly lead to learning, and the students see this growth in their learning, relevancy is built, and autonomy begins to bloom—yet another step in moving those students from dependent (*What are we doing?)* to independent (*I understand!*).

We are a very assessment-heavy culture in the education system right now, and while we can't fight that, it also can't become the main focus from day one of the school year. If we are setting meaningful learning goals that are aligned to the expectations of the state, the assessments won't have to be the end goal. Learning to think at the level the assessments will require, and learning the skills that the state laid out for that content and grade level, will be the goal. The assessment will just measure the learning.

Once the clear learning target is defined, and you have determined how students will show you that they have mastered it, teachers should then, *and only then*, plan for the student tasks. These tasks should have a direct impact on the learning. Remember the learner's brain we discussed in Chapter 2? Every task we design for our students should deepen the groove in that neural pathway of the new learning.

What types of tasks tend to deepen the groove? As you choose tasks, I would look for the following characteristics.

Do the tasks:

- Use a wide range of learning modalities (visual, kinesthetic, auditory)

- Allow students the opportunity to process and make connections

- Build and utilize all four language domains (students are reading, writing, speaking and listening)

You should be able to ask yourself, "If the student completes this task, will it directly lead to learning and impact student mastery of the learning target?" If it doesn't, then the task needs to be reevaluated.

There will be times when your answer to this question, as you are planning, is "yes," but then the formative assessment tells a different story. That's okay! You can adjust your instruction moving forward, and you lose very little learning time. This situation just affirms the importance of the ongoing formative assessment.

WHAT DO I GRADE?

I want to address a very common question. I know that most districts require a certain number of grades in the gradebook, but let's talk about when it is appropriate to take a grade.

In Chapter 2, we addressed the importance of making learning the focus and not a grade. Even if students shoot their hands up to ask the inevitable, "Miss, is this for a grade?" we cannot be tricked into thinking this is their only leverage for learning. If we have introduced new learning, and then give a task and immediately tell the students it's for a grade, we will have stifled the "productive struggle" for many students just trying to get the grade.

Students must have the opportunity to process, problem solve, debate, or work out the correct answer. If they have 20 minutes to complete an assignment for a grade, they may not have the time to go through this process. This is a leading contributor to keeping students dependent learners, and will inevitably lead to other behaviors, such as copying or shutting down. Grades should only be taken on tasks that students have had adequate time and tasks to learn the new material.

I want to caution you on giving "participation" grades. As a mother, if my son has a 92 average in reading, I'm assuming that he's doing fine in the skill of reading and reading comprehension. If he brings home a 60 on a test, that's going to be a red flag to me. However, if he has had adequate time to learn and practice the skill, and his grade average is between a 60 and 70, that lets me know as a parent where his skill level is, and what he needs to work on.

If you work with older students, giving them a participation grade can also give them a false sense of security. Once they get an "I'm

doing fine in math class" mentality, even if they actually need additional help, their intrinsic motivation to work harder may be skewed due to a false sense of accomplishment.

I absolutely believe that students should be affirmed for participation and effort, but I would recommend specific praise, classroom privileges, or positive contacts home instead of number grades in the gradebook.

Differentiation

> "At its most basic level, differentiated instruction means "shaking up" what goes on in the classroom so that students have multiple options for taking in information, making sense of ideas, and expressing what they learn." [3]

So how do we set common, grade level learning targets for all students to hit when we have so many different levels of students, both academically and linguistically, sitting in the same class? The answer is differentiation.

I want to stop right here with a caveat—teaching is one of the most noble professions, and noble professions are not easy.

> *"The heartbreaking difficulty in pedagogy, as indeed in*
> *medicine and other branches of knowledge that partake*
> *at the same time of art and science, is, in fact,*
> *that the best methods are also the most difficult ones."*
> **— Jean Piaget**

Differentiation is not easy, and it takes planning, but it is necessary and doable when done correctly.

What differentiation *is*	What differentiation *is not*
Proactive	It is not a separate assignment for each student
Qualitative more than quantitative	It is not separate lessons for each student
Student-centered	It is not different academic expectations for each student
Rooted in assessment	
Blend of whole-class, group, and individual instruction	It is not chaotic
Provides multiple approaches	It is not homogeneous grouping
	It is not making assignments harder or easier
	It is not only for struggling students

Differentiation is typically broken down into different parts:

- Context
- Process
- Product[3]

The context directly relates to culturally responsive teaching. This is the understanding that students bring different contextual backgrounds to the classroom, and if we want to make the content relevant, we must address the different contexts. There are many ways to do this. Some are:

- Texts—stories, articles, word problems
- Examples

- Building background to develop and determine the students' schema prior to teaching the content

The <u>process</u> is the way in which the information is given and learned. There are seemingly endless ways to differentiate the process, but here are some examples:

- Hands on learning
- Videos
- Notetaking
- Graphic organizers
- Visuals
- Writing
- Speaking
- Cooperative learning
- Reading comprehension strategies

It is important to note again that differentiation is proactive and not just for struggling students. Differentiation occurs in the first-teach, meaning that as you plan your instruction for all students, you plan for the information to be given and received through several different processes. You may show a short video to introduce a concept, give a graphic organizer for the students to take notes, and have the students talk through the content with a partner, and then use visuals to match meanings. With this instruction you have hit many different learning styles and language proficiencies, and you will drastically cut down on the amount of reteaching that needs to occur.

The <u>product</u> is the way that the students show their mastery of

the learning. This can be done through choice boards, use of technology, different domains of output in learning (writing, speaking), making lists, labeling pictures or graphs, graphic organizers, multiple choice, etc.

I love to write. I write to think. I can make decisions, make sense of my thoughts, and communicate better through writing. I soared through my master's program because the majority of it was writing. This was my output of choice; therefore, it was easy to show my learning. Writing is not necessarily the output of choice for everyone (some of you reading this are probably raising your hand right now). It's not that you haven't learned the content. It's just that writing would not be your preferred way to show your learning.

Our students are the same way. Some of them would prefer to make a video, others would prefer to write, others would prefer to speak their answers, and still others may prefer to show their learning artistically. While it's not feasible to always have product choices (after all, they will eventually have to take a standardized test), throughout the learning process, it is important to differentiate the way the students show their learning.

Here is an example of brainstorming for a specific learning objective.

Learning target: Compare and classify living and nonliving things

Context	Process	Product
Build background, show visuals of possible unknown environments.	Have students brainstorm living and nonliving things with a group.	Draw pictures.
Ask students from different regions ahead of time and research living things.	Students and teacher create an anchor chart to compare living and nonliving.	Word sort.
Use the school environment as the first-teach example.	Students use the anchor chart to determine living or non-living— check their thought with a partner and hold up an "L" or "N".	Write explanations using sentence frames.
	Students create a non-linguistic representation to "take notes" on living or non-living. They could label.	Create a new environment and explain what living and nonliving things would be found there.

Vocabulary

Vocabulary is the key to comprehension. Research has shown that first-grade children from higher-SES groups knew about twice as many words as lower SES children. In addition, a study of 165 college freshmen enrolled in a remedial reading course found that vocabulary was the only variable that made a statistically significant contribution to measures of literal and critical reading comprehension, evaluation and appreciation of reading materials.[4]

How do we help these students when they come in with such a deficit? How do we fill in these gaps?

We do it with intentional, explicit, interactive vocabulary instruction!

What does that look like? Does it look like students writing down definitions and writing them in a sentence? Does it look like a student spending a large chunk of time to illustrate one word? Does it look like students looking up words in a dictionary or glossary?

Going back to the learning, my question in determining vocabulary instruction would be, "Do these tasks lead to learning?" If they do, keep doing them! But my guess is that students could spend 45 minutes writing down definitions and using the words in a sentence and come back the next day unable to give the meaning of very many of the words.

Many of these students are lacking the background knowledge and the academic language needed to add new vocabulary seamlessly. They need to have the words in context, interact with the words, see the words, hear the words, play games with the words, and manipulate the words.

Here are some, what I would call, *non-negotiables* when it comes to vocabulary:

- Have the words posted and visual. This could be a word wall, anchor chart, or list. The students need to see the words repeatedly. Point to the word whenever you use it in class.

- Repetition. Students need to hear and say the words many times.

- Play games. When students are engaged and having fun, learning increases. (See Book Study)

- Teach word parts. Teach the prefix, suffix or root words to increase the meaning and build the capacity for learning new words.

Some vocabulary issues to look out for are:

- Assessment words. This can be a language all on its own. The students need to be familiar with the words and language of the assessments. Any words that you don't hear in the hallway is a vocabulary word and needs to be taught!

- Multi-meaning words. These words can be very tricky for our struggling students and English learners. Explicitly teaching them can be very helpful.

Overarching vocabulary strategies:

- Cognates. For your students who are literate in another Latin-based language, having them identify words that look or sound the same in English as they do in their native language is great strategy.

- Total physical response. This is putting movement to or using hand motion with a meaning. Having this physical motion connect to a meaning has a huge impact on learning.

- Context clues. Although using a dictionary or looking up a word is a strategy, using context clues is often the best way to determine the meaning of an unfamiliar word. Teaching your students this meta-cognitive skill can help them across content areas as well.

Intentional, planned, targeted instruction is imperative for your students in need of culturally responsive teaching. Clear targets, formative assessments and feedback, aligned tasks, differentiation, and intentional vocabulary instruction are the perfect formula for designing the meaningful instruction that these students so desperately want and need.

Chapter 7 At a Glance

Intentional instruction can be broken down into five different parts:

1. Clear learning targets
2. Feedback and formative assessment
3. Aligned and meaningful tasks
4. Differentiation
5. Vocabulary

Set clear learning targets based on the standard EVERY DAY. Students and teacher should have clarity on the learning. Formative assessments should consistently measure the learning.

Tasks should be meaningful and relevant, and should directly facilitate the students mastering the learning goal.

Differentiation can occur in the context of the learning, the process of the instruction, and the product the students create to show mastery.

What differentiation *is*:

- Proactive
- Qualitative more than quantitative
- Student-centered
- Rooted in assessment
- Blend of whole-class, group, and individual instruction
- Provides multiple approaches

Non-negotiables when it comes to vocabulary:

1. Words should be posted and visual
2. Repetition
3. Play games
4. Teach word parts

Let's Process

1. How do you ensure you have teacher clarity? Can you and your students answer these three questions each day?

   a. What are you learning?

   b. Why are you learning it?

   c. How will you know when you learned it?

2. Do the tasks you create for the students directly lead to their learning?

3. Do the students find these tasks relevant and meaningful? Are they engaged?

4. How do you measure the learning each day?

5. How do you differentiate the context? The process? The product?

6. How are you teaching vocabulary? Is it filling in the language gaps for your struggling students?

Strategies for Implementation
Culturally Responsive Teaching Checklist — See Appendix

Favorite Resources on This Topic
Academic Vocabulary for English Learners, EL Saber Enterprises[5]

STAAR Guide to Success, EL Saber Enterprises[6]

How to Differentiate Instruction in Mixed-Ability Classrooms, Carol Ann Tomlinson[3]

PART IV
Teacher Talk

"Teachers, I believe, are the most responsible and important members of society because their professional efforts affect the fate of the earth."

HELEN CALDICOTT

*T*here will never be enough words of appreciation to truly match the work of a teacher—especially a culturally responsive teacher who is willing to put in the work, dedication, self-reflection and love to reach his or her students. I am fortunate enough to be surrounded by several of these, and I wanted their voices to be heard as well.

Each of these teachers, or administrators, are experts in their own rights in one or more areas of being culturally responsive, and they were kind enough to share that expertise with me.

Amy White is an eighth grade ELA teacher in North Richland Hills, Texas. As we worked together on culturally responsive teaching, she really grasped hold of the importance of alignment and cooperative learning. She intentionally started releasing control of her class and allowed them the time to have the productive struggle, which built success in her class. Out of 160 students, 130 passed (with many of the 30 who didn't pass seeing the online test for the first time). Even for those who didn't pass the first administration, there was an average of a 20% jump on their score!

1. *How difficult was it for you to remove yourself from immediately helping a student?*
It was extremely difficult at the beginning. When I look around my room and see them struggling, I want to make them feel like, "I got this." So it was hard for me to take myself out of the picture and let them be responsible for their own learning.

2. *What did you put into place to help students problem-solve?*
The biggest were the scaffolds. Scaffolding of instructions and tasks. Chunking the assignment—think time first, now write your answer, now discuss. Instead of me giving them the right answer or immediately telling them, "You're not on the right train of thought."

3. *When you started making that shift, how did your kids respond at first?*
At first, they weren't very happy because they were used to me jumping in and giving them the answer. After they got used to it, they started to enjoy it. Participation increased because no one wanted to be the person that was just sitting in their seat because they didn't get their pre-work thinking done. This also helped with behavior. Even in the class where kids didn't want to do the work because it wasn't the 'cool thing' to do, they eventually came around.

4. *How were you planning previously, and what were the results?*
Looking briefly at the standard, determining the concept ("theme"), determining the definition of that concept and teach that concept through an activity. Very activity-based. We just weren't seeing the growth on the activities.

5. *How are you planning now, and what are the results?*
The way we're planning now is reading the entire standard, breaking it down by what they need to know and what they need to do, then pulling the vocabulary. We then pull the released questions on the state assessment to build the question stems so that we are sure we are using the vocabulary that they are going to see. So by the time they see the questions, they are not surprised by the questions.

6. *How are you currently using cooperative learning, and what are you seeing now?*
We used cooperative learning to increase engagement. We would read the passage, they would respond on their own individually, then they would discuss with another person either at their table or with

another person at a different table (to get more perspective). We then moved from short answers to multiple choices. Students really stayed engaged, and the more we did it, the better the conversations.

7. What did you see as one of the biggest challenges of having such a diverse classroom?
Getting every student where they needed to be—reading levels, vocabulary, being closer to grade level. Setting clear goals for growth for each student. Students were not motivated, students not having the "buy-in"—"I haven't cared yet, not going to care now."

8. What are your students saying about the way you are running your classroom now and the learning that they are accomplishing?
The students love it. They haven't gotten burned out. The students keep asking, "Can we do it like we did yesterday?" They feel good about learning. I kept asking, "Do you feel like you can pass this test?" They responded, "Yes! We actually feel confident!"

Overall observations:
One of the biggest things I learned is really making them be the learners—making them do the hard work even though it is really hard. I think this has been my most successful year of teaching. I went from guessing that it was the right thing to teach to having a target. My confidence overall as a teacher has increased and I enjoy it so much more.

Tyra Sentell, M.Ed has served as an Assistant Principal and Instructional Reading Specialist at the elementary level. She has worked in many different types of schools and is an expert at teaching reading and coaching.

1. As an administrator, what is the direct relationship between behavior issues and teacher relationships with students?
Hand in hand. When you have the relationship built with students, it's a direct correlation to the level of behavior. When you have been intentional with the relationship, you will not see the ongoing and repetitive problems. The students trust the teacher.

2. As an administrator/instructional coach, what would you say are the top three things classroom teachers can do to promote learning?
Relationship, planning engaging and intentional lessons, and student-run classrooms where students are in charge of their learning.

3. What are some common phrases that you hear from students when they are sent to the office repeatedly for behavior issues?
"I'll be back."

When you send your students to the office, you're sending your authority with them.

4. *Based on data, have you noticed the "type" of classroom and/or teacher that seems to promote learning the most?*
The teacher has high expectations and created a safe environment where students feel safe to ask and risk questions.

5. *Working in several different schools, have you seen different leverage points (positive or negative) for different sub-populations? (For example, grades, parent phone calls, rewards, teacher relationships, ISS, etc.)*
In lower SES schools, I've seen teachers try to use intimidation or fear to keep students compliant and keep a hold of classroom management, but without the trust the students so desperately need, this method does not lead to learning. Trust between the teacher and the student and the parents is necessary to manage behavior and facilitate learning.

6. *What are your overall observations of children coming from lower socio-economic status (SES) families, and middle or upper SES families?*
The families come with the expectation that the school will take care of 100% of education.

7. *What are some of the skills children from lower SES families bring to the classroom (assertiveness, life skills, leadership on the playground, etc.)?*
Survival Skills—resilience in life situations.

8. *What are some of the academic deficits or gaps of children from lower SES families seem to bring to the classroom (vocabulary, phonics, etc.)?*
Foundational skills—academic.

Jared Gibson is a seventh grade pre-AP teacher in Watauga, Texas. He has been extremely intentional in creating a student-centered environment, where students take ownership of their learning and their class. He does a fantastic job of building an alliance with the students and creating a "family" environment within each class.

1. *What challenges were you seeing in your classroom that led you to tackle the alliance and "tribe" community?*
My first couple of years was "all me." I was doing everything and not getting the grades and the class participation I wanted. After attending professional development (specifically, the Ron Clark Academy), it showed me that teaching was about empowering the kids and letting them take the lead.

2. *How have you seen this adjustment in the climate affect learning?*
It's definitely affected the learning. Looking at the data—my Curriculum Based Assessment (CBA) average was around 33% and I heard my students say things like, "I've never seen this information before." That hurt. But giving them the leadership roles, now they take more ownership of their behavior and their learning because their actions affect their classmates. CBAs are high-80s now. The cooperative learning helps the students understand the content coming through from a peer. They are responsible for their own learning and teaching each other leads to better understanding of the concepts.

3. *What are strategies you've put into place specifically to build an alliance between you and your students?*

I've tried to build a "we're on the same team" mentality. Giving students specific leadership roles, like a president and vice president in the class that I pick—they have to show me that they want to have that role; this builds trust between us. They also have special leadership privileges, like better seats, don't have to ask to go to the bathroom, and they get to go to the class party, the reward for earning the most points, regardless of if their class won in order to motivate them to create leadership. We are working together to build their leadership. I have created the attitude of "I will trust you until you break it."

4. *What are strategies you've put into place to build the tribe?*

The house system, the positive points—students shake hands at the door, lead PowerPoint presentations, take roll— intentionally build respectful interactions, starting with "present, Mr. President"— helping others, being kind, highest GPA as a class—encourage studying and respectfulness.

5. *How has this "tribal climate" encouraged cooperative learning?*

I would say the primary thing I've been intentional about was teaching the students how to speak to each other, and then giving lots of chances to practice in low stress situations. I changed the seating arrangements, and I've noticed kids are relating to each other better. I frontload the instructions sometimes and let kids lead the notes. Kids are practicing their speaking in front of class, and their confidence builds to be able to be in cooperative learning because they've already

had the interactions. I always explain the expectations, modeled the appropriate responses and speaking, and reward house points to responses.

April Mueller was my son's wonderful first grade teacher in North Richland Hills, Texas. She is currently working as a 5th grade teacher in Weldon Spring, Missouri. Her strength is filling in the achievement gaps in the primary grades, holding the students to high expectations, and creating a warm, family-like environment. She gave my son a love for learning, took him from a "bubble student" right on the cusp of not being at grade level in reading, and moved him into being above grade level. She built a family feel within the class, and the students genuinely felt her love.

1. *What are your overall observations of children who come from lower socio-economic status (SES) families and middle or upper SES families?*
Most of my lower SES students love the structure and consistency of school. The predictability and safe environment help put them at ease. Some of these families seem to be under extra stress.

2. *What are some of the skills children from lower SES families bring to the classroom (assertiveness, life skills, leadership on the playground, etc.)?*
I find that some of these students bring extra motivation and determination. They come with grit. I also find that they can be more tolerant of troubled or difficult children.

3. What are some of the academic deficits or gaps the children from lower SES families seem to bring to the classroom (vocabulary, phonics, etc.)?
I have found gaps in resources. They may not have pencils, papers, crayons and books at home. I also see a deficit in vocabulary and life experiences (having visited a beach, gone to a museum, seen a play, etc.). Their background knowledge sometimes lacks heft.

4. What are your observations of family involvement?
Some lower SES families are busy with work and have less time to support their children academically and emotionally. I have found some families are very dedicated to classroom achievement and work with their children faithfully.

5. How have you intentionally helped the family become involved in their student's learning?
I meet with families in person at the beginning of the school year to establish good communication and trust. If needed, I provide resources for families to use with their children at home and train them on simple exercises. When students make progress, I love sharing this news with families, so that they can celebrate and feel motivated to continue support. I send all my children home with appropriate reading material.

6. How do you differentiate instruction for students who come with varying levels of language and vocabulary?
I check-in with students more frequently to be sure that they are understanding the material. We read books, watch videos and have peer discussions to help students gain some background knowledge

of subjects. At times, I use sentence stems so that students have support in beginning a discussion about a topic.

7. How much do you focus on social-emotional development and interpersonal skills?

Every day it is my goal to make the day great for my students. I want them to know that they are loved and celebrated. It is incredibly important for me to build a classroom with positive culture so that all students can thrive. The classroom provides endless opportunities to model problem-solving and best practices. My classroom is a safe place for kids to "fail" socially and have a chance to make better choices in the future. Children learn best when they are happy and engaged.

8. Are students aware of the specific standards you are teaching, and do they track their progress? If so, how?

Yes! Our TEKS are found on our anchor charts and explicitly talked about as a class. We have goals each week that we track on bulletin boards and in data folders. We have goals for the year, as well as goals for the week.

Aristo Torres, M. Ed is a Principal of a K–5 charter school in Dallas, Texas. He is a master at relationship building, and leading his teachers to do the same, while helping to put structures and expectations into place to facilitate learning.

1. *As an administrator, what is the direct relationship between behavior issues and teacher relationships with students?*

The classroom should be a collaboration, not a dictatorship. If you want good classroom management, there has to be a relationship. Teachers that send students to the office do not have a relationship with the students. The office should be the last point, because every time the student goes to the office, the teacher has to reestablish a relationship.

2. *As an administrator, what would you say are the top three things classroom teachers can do to promote learning?*

Build rapport.

　　Classroom management — have structures and procedures.

　　Accountability — have expectations—goal sheet.

3. *What are some common phrases that you hear from students when they are sent to the office repeatedly for behavior issues?*

"It was not me."

　　"She (the teacher) doesn't like me."

　　"I was not the only one."

4. *Based on data, have you noticed the "type" of classroom and/or teacher that seems to promote learning the most?*
In a self-run classroom, the teacher works with a small group. The rest of the class knows what they're doing. They are operating on their own. It is student-centered.

5. *What are your overall observations of children who come from lower socio-economic status (SES) families and middle or upper SES families?*
The majority of parents who are educated, the students follow the trend. Students tend to follow the trend of the parents.

Hard working parents in low SES push their students to work hard. They can be encouragers, but they often can't help their students academically.

Scott Drue, M.Ed and **Alfonso Giardiello, M.Ed** the Principal
and Vice Principal, respectively, of Aloha-Huber Park School (K–8)
in Beaverton, Oregon. This school is the epitome of a lower SES
school that has moved students from dependent to independent
learners with a very systemic approach to building relationships with
the students and offering equitable curriculum and instruction for
all students. I invite you to follow these two rock star administrators
on their journey from taking this underperforming school to being
number six out of 33 elementary schools in Beaverton, and representing the only Title I school in the top 15 schools in the district. (See
www.leadersofequity.org.)

1. *As administrators, what is the direct relationship between behavior
issues and teacher relationships with students?*
It is 100% directly proportional. Our first guiding principle states
that all adult actions impact student learning, whether that's negative
or positive. We believe very strongly in building community.

2. As administrators, what would you say are the top three things class-room teachers can do to promote learning?

Take a systems approach to build the relationship. Teachers team, plan and commonly assess as a team. No matter what teacher they get, all instruction is quality. We hire well to ensure a strong team. Great schools must have great leadership. We strategize often. We find a good teacher to fit in the culture of the school first, and we have clear statements and non-negotiables. We provide clear support and affirmations.

3. What are some common phrases that you hear from students when they are sent to the office repeatedly for behavior issues?

Currently, we don't have students sent to the office. Ever.

Back in 2006, maintaining behavior was a full-time job, and we mainly heard, "Wasn't me."

Now kids are working through problems and explaining how they are going to make it right. We use restorative practices.

4. Based on data, have you noticed the type of classroom and/or teacher that seems to promote learning the most?

Data-driven classrooms where instruction is guided by formative assessment is best. A teacher willing to be in a team approach works the best. When there is a plan for kids who didn't do well on an assessment, the entire team makes a plan, even if one teacher didn't have any students who didn't perform well. Everyone contributes.

5. What are some of the skills children from lower SES families bring to the classroom (assertiveness, life skills, leadership on the playground, etc.)?
They bring a sense of resilience, a love of community, an ability to connect and create the family unit, and exposure and acceptance to many different ethnicities.

6. What are some of the academic deficits or gaps children from lower SES families seem to bring to the classroom (vocabulary, phonics, etc.)?
Ninety percent don't know letter sounds or letter sense in kindergarten.

7. What are the primary ways your staff reaches your ELs?
Creating independent learners. Heavy on the scaffolding at early ages.

8. How have your teachers promoted a student-centered classroom?
Assess and personalize learning early on to have every student on grade level by first grade. Build fundamentals.

The pathway to student independence is modeling the steps they should take. Do not assume they know. It's an intentional process.

Conclusion

*T*eaching is hard. Teaching a diverse group of students is hard. Loving your students to the point where you are losing sleep over them at night is hard. Trying to meet their academic, social and emotional needs is hard. Trying to pull in the students and families that are hopeless is hard. Trying to get students to meet the level of thinking and rigor is hard. There's no way to get around it. Teaching is hard!

But now we know it's possible. We have the steps and strategies needed to create the environment and instruction that leads to academic success!

When we embrace the mindset that not every student has an equal opportunity at education, but that we have the control over the climate and learning that happens in our classroom, we will be more apt to build the environment the students need to overcome the challenges so many of them are bringing to the classroom.

We will understand the difference between the collectivist and individualist culture and create instruction that motivates and engages both cultures.

We will set high expectations and model and practice the behavior we expect. We will provide a supportive environment that builds autonomy, but we won't run in and "rescue" students when they have a question. We'll allow the productive struggle, but in a safe environment where risk-taking is the norm.

We'll build a tribal community where we teach the students how to connect with each other and value each other by first showing that we value them. We will build an alliance, set common goals, create tasks that help our students meet those goals, and then celebrate the journey!

In closing, we lead with love, but empower with knowledge. We look at situations for what they are. If a student has shut down or is acting out, instead of reacting emotionally, we look at it as learned helplessness, begin lowering the affective, build autonomy, move the student back into being an independent learner. We consider how the brain learns and we dig the neural grooves needed for real learning.

And lastly, we embrace the different experiences and deep culture that our students are bringing into the classroom. We structure our environment and instruction to powerfully create independent learners with the beautiful students we have been entrusted to teach.

Thank you for going on this journey with me.

Appendix

Cultural Survey

1. How did your family identify ethnically or racially?

2. Where did you live-urban, suburban or rural community?

3. What is the story of your family in America? Has your family been here for generations or a few years?

4. How would you describe your family's economic status—middle class, upper class, working class, or low income? What did that mean in terms of quality of life?

5. Were you the first in your family to attend college? If not, who did?

6. What stories did you hear growing up?

7. List some family traditions—holidays, food, rituals.

8. Who were heroes celebrated in your family? Who were the "antiheroes?"

9. What were some "sayings" that you heard throughout your family growing up? What did they mean?

10. What did respect look like? Disrespect?

11. How were you trained to respond to different emotional displays—crying, anger, and happiness?

12. What physical, social, or cultural attributes were praised in your community? Which were you taught to avoid?

13. How were you expected to interact with authority figures? Was authority of teachers and other elders assumed or did it have to be earned?

14. As a child, did you call adults by their first name?

15. What got you shunned or shamed in your family? What earned you praise?

16. Were you allowed to question adults?

17. What's your family/community's relationship with time?

18. How were you expected to perform in school?

19. Were you given tangible rewards to performing in school, doing chores, etc, or were you expected to take care of responsibility?

20. In your classroom (life), what behaviors do you expect your students or children to exhibit?

21. What were you taught about reasons other racial or ethnic groups succeeded or not?

22. Did you grow up thinking that people were born with intelligence?

23. Did you grow up believing that some groups are smarter than others?

24. How important is religion in your life, and do you believe it should be the foundation for others' lives?

*A copy-friendly version of this survey can be found in the Book Study Appendix.

Cultural Survey — Students

1. How does your family identify ethnically or racially?

2. Where do you live-urban, suburban or rural community?

3. What is the story of your family in America? Has your family been here for generations or a few years?

4. Is college a goal of yours? Would you be the first person in your family to go to college? If not, who went to college?

5. List some family traditions—holidays, food, rituals.

6. Who are heroes celebrated in your family? Who are the "antiheroes?"

7. What does respect look like? Disrespect?

8. What is the appropriate way to respond to different emotional displays—crying, anger, and happiness—in your family?

9. How are you expected to interact with authority figures? Is authority of teachers and other elders assumed or does it have to be earned?

10. Were you allowed to question adults?

11. What's your family/community's relationship with time?

12. How are you expected to perform in school?

13. Are you given tangible rewards to performing in school, doing chores, etc., or were you expected to take care of responsibility?

14. What were you taught about reasons other racial or ethnic groups succeeded or not?

15. Do you think that people are born with intelligence?

16. How important is religion in your life, and do you believe it should be the foundation for others' lives?

*A copy-friendly version of this survey can be found in the Book Study Appendix.

Voice Chart

Voice	Description	Strategies
V	Visuals	• Pictures • Realia • Videos • Anchor charts • Word walls • Posted directions
O	Oracy: "the ability to express oneself fluently and grammatically correct" (www.dictionary.com) academic dialogue, speaking about specific content	• Inside-outside circle • Think-pair-share-write • Turn and talk • Question stems / response frames • Cooperative learning
I	Interactive Vocabulary: specifically and intentionally facilitating students to interact with vocabulary terms through conversation, games, and manipulation of words and meanings	• Interactive word wall games: musical words, unfolding 5 words in a story, draw me • Concept definition maps • Open or Closed Word Sorts
C	Comprehension: understanding new information (orally or through text) in a given content area	• Survey Technique • Picture It
E	Evaluation of Language	• Goal setting with students • Rubrics based on TELPAS

Culturally Responsive Teaching Checklist

In the planning:

☐   1. Start with the standard.

☐   2. What do the students have to **know**? What do the students have to **do**?

☐   3. Determine the vocabulary and teach explicitly.

☐   4. Create questions that are at the level of thinking required of the students to master the standard.

☐   5. Create activities that answer the question: "Does this activity lead my students to master the standard?"

6. Scaffold for strugglers:

a) Pre-teach vocabulary.

b) Model the thinking.

☐ c) Build up the level of questions (start with level 1 and work up).

d) Chunk the reading (*but require student reading*).

e) Use sentence frames for conversation and/or writing.

☐ 7. Provide a formative assessment with immediate feedback.

In the classroom:

☐ 1. Make sure vocabulary is visual.

☐ 2. Post directions and procedures.

☐ 3. Post learning goal for the day and refer to it.

☐ 4. Create and implement a way for students to get help (a part from you and always a neighbor).

☐ 5. Consider the gradual release model: You Do (You model), We Do (you and the students think together), We Do Together (cooperative learning where they think together), and I Do (individual work).

☐ 6. Facilitate academic interaction—they need to discuss the learning!

☐ 7. Provide anchor charts, graphic organizers, or notes for students to refer to when doing cooperative learning and individual work.

☐ 8. Provide *wait time* for processing and language.

☐ 9. Consider the collectivist vs. individualistic cultures—are grades the end goal? (This won't motivate many of your students.)

☐ 10. Provide structures and processes for the higher structure classes.

In the alliance:

☐   1. Does every student know you care?

☐   2. Do you have a particular way you greet each student?

☐   3. Have you made positive contact with their parents or guardians?

☐   4. Do you understand the collectivist mindset?
      a) Friends and family come first.
      b) Education may not be top priority.
      c) Relationships come before learning.

☐   5. Do you have common goals?

*A copy-friendly version of this survey can be found in the Book Study Appendix.

Notes

CHAPTER 1

1. Culture. (n.d) retrieved from www.people.tamu.edu/~i-choudhury/culture.

2. Darling, Sandra K. and Donna W. Tileston, *Why Culture Counts*. Bloomington: Solution Tree Press, 2008. pp 25.

3. *Marriage and Family Encyclopedia*: Asian families. (n.d) retrieved from www.family.jrank.org/pages/103/Asian-American-Families-Family -Structures-Gender-Roles.

4. Cherry, Kendra. (2018, Oct 31) Understanding Collectivist Cultures: How Culture Can Influence Behavior, retrieved from www.verywellmind.com /what-are-collectivistic-cultures-2794962.

5. Galanti, Geri Ann. (n.d) retrieved from www.ggalanti.org/cultural-diversity-in-healthcare.

6. Zusak, Markus. *The Book Thief*. New York: Alfred A. Knopf, 2005.

7. www.verywellmind.com/what-are-collectivistic-cultures-2794962.

8. Cherry, Kendra. (2019, Jul 26) Individualistic Cultures and Behaviors, retrieved from www.verywellmind.com/what-are-individualistic-cultures-2795273.

9. Hammond, Zaretta. *Culturally Responsive Teaching and the Brain*. Thousand Oaks: Corwin, 2015. pp 31, 33.

10. *Academic Vocabulary for English Learners,* EL Saber Enterprises, 2019.

CHAPTER 2

1. Smith, Belle. (2019, May 04) Why Is There A Huge Academic-Achievement Gap Between White Students And Their Peers Of Color? Retrieved from www.parentherald.com/articles/41239/20160504 /why-is-there-a-huge-academic-achievement-gap-between-white -students-and-their-peers-of-color.htm.

2. Reardon, Sean F. et al. (2018). Stanford Education Data Archive (Version 2.1). http://purl.stanford.edu/db586ns4974.

3. Hammond, Zaretta. *Culturally Responsive Teaching and the Brain.* Thousand Oaks: Corwin, 2015. Print.

4. Vasquez, Veronica. (n.d) Lowering the affective filter for English language learners facilitates successful language acquisition. Chart adapted from www.collaborativeclassroom.org/blog/lowering-the-affective-filter-for -english-language-learners-facilitates-successful-language-acquisition.

5. Seligman, Martin (2006). Learned optimism: How to change your mind and your life. New York: Vintage.

6. Rugnetta, Michael (n.d) Neuroplasticity. Retrieved from https://www .britannica.com/science/neuroplasticity.

7. Darling, Sandra K. and Donna W. Tileston, *Why Culture Counts.* Bloomington: Solution Tree Press, 2008. Print.

8. Jenson, Eric. *The Learning Brain.* San Diego: Turning Point Publishing, 1995. Print.

9. *Stra-tiques: Flip Into Success.* EL Saber Enterprises, 2011.

10. Kagan, S. and M. Kagan. *Kagan Cooperative Learning,* San Clemente: Kagan Publishing, 2009.

11. The Condition of Education: Last updated: May 2019; https://nces.ed.gov /programs/coe/indicator_coi.asp.

CHAPTER 3

1. Tatum, Alfred. *Teaching Reading to Black Adolescent Males: Closing the Achievement Gap*. Portland: Stenhouse Publishers, 2005. pp 12, 15, 32.

2. Minor, Cornelius. *We Got This: Equity, Access, and the Quest to Be Who Our Students Need Us to Be*. Portsmouth, 2017.

3. Hammond, Zaretta. *Culturally Responsive Teaching and the Brain*. Thousand Oaks: Corwin, 2015. pp 31, 33.

4. Dyson, M. E. *Holler If You Hear Me: Searching for Tupac Shakir*. New York: Basic Civitas Books, 2001.

5. Darling, Sandra K. and Donna W. Tileston, *Why Culture Counts*. Bloomington: Solution Tree Press, 2008. Print. pp 67, 68, 69, 73, 165.

6. United States Department of Education. Our nation's English Learners. What are their characteristics? Retrieved from www2.ed.gov/datastory /el-characteristics/index.html.

7. The Latino Family Literacy Project. 2019. James Cummins' theory of second language acquisition. Retrieved from https://www.latinoliteracy.com /james-cummins-theory-second-language-acquisition/.

8. Kreisa, Meredith. 2019. The FluentU. The Dreaded Language Learning Plateau: How to Rise Above It. Retrieved from www.fluentu.com/blog /language-learning-plateau/.

9. Random House Dictionary. 2019. Retrieved from www.dictionary.com /browse/oracy.

10. VOICE Chart for LTELs. EL Saber Enterprises (2018).

11. Henderson, N., & Milstein N.M. *Resiliency in Schools: Making it Happen for Students and Educators*, Thousand Oaks: Corwin Press. 1996.

12. *Stra-tiques: Flip Into Success*. EL Saber Enterprises, 2011.

13. DOK Question Stems and Response Frames. EL Saber Enterprises, 2018.

14. *Academic Vocabulary for English Learners,* EL Saber Enterprises, 2019.

CHAPTER 4

1. Aoki's World. (2016, Mar 29) Forty Really Best Quotes about Teacher. Retrieved from http://quoteideas.com/teacher-quotes.

2. Jenson, Eric. *Teaching with Poverty in Mind.* Alexandria: ASCD, 2009. pp 9, 45.

3. US Census Bureau, 2000. Retrieved from https://www.census.gov /census2000/states/us.html.

4. Drue, Scott and Giardiello, A. (2019, Apr 11) The Road to Guaranteed and Viable Curriculum. Retrieved from https://www.leadersofequity.org /data-outcomes.

5. Scott, Elizabeth (2019, Jul 29) 17 Highly Effective Stress Relievers. Retrieved from https://www.verywellmind.com/tips-to-reduce-stress-3145195.

6. Darling, S. and D. Tileston. *Why Culture Counts: Teaching Children of Poverty.* Bloomington: 2008. Solution Tree Press.

7. Jenson, Eric. *The Learning Brain.* San Diego: Turning Point Publishing, 1995. Print.

8. Payne, Ruby K. and Paul D. Slocumb. *Boys in Poverty.* Bloomington: Solution Tree Press, 2011. Print.

CHAPTER 5

1. Random House Dictionary. 2019. Retrieved from www.dictionary.com /browse/alliance.

2. Fisher, Douglas, Frey, N. and R. Qualia. *Engagement by Design.* Thousand Oaks: Corwin, 2018. Print.

3. http://www.lacoe.edu/schoolimprovement/statefederalprograms

/sfppublications. aspx,(Los Angeles County Office of Education, 2002, p D-31).

4. Hammond, Zaretta. *Culturally Responsive Teaching and the Brain.* Thousand Oaks: Corwin, 2015. Print. pp 33.

5. DeAngelis, Tori (2008, Feb) Vol 39, No 2, pp 30. The two faces of oxytocin. American Psychology Association. Retrieved from www.apa.org/monitor /feb08/oxytocin.

6. Lahey, Jessica (2015, Jan 23) Should teachers be allowed to touch students? Retrieved from https://www.theatlantic.com/education/archive/2015/01 /the-benefits-of-touch/ 384706/.

7. Burchard, B. "Best Of: How to Influence an Underperformer." Podcast: *The Brendon Show.* 6 May, 2019.

8. Burchard, Brendon. *High Performance Habits.* New York: Hay House Inc, 2017.

9. Kleiber, Jennifer (2019, May 17) 4 Steps to Influence the Underperformer— and start the move past learned helplessness.www.pressing-onward.org — blog.

CHAPTER 6

1. Jenson, Eric. *Teaching with Poverty in Mind.* Alexandria: ASCD, 2009.

2. Sprick, Randy. *CHAMPS: A Proactive Approach to Classroom Management.* Safe and Civil Schools. Eugene, OR: Northwest Pacific. 2009.

3. Everlove, Sandi, Fisher, D., and Frey, N. *Productive Group Work.* Alexandria: ASCD, 2009. Print. pp 19.

4. Kleiber, Jennifer (2018, Jan 29) The power of conversation—from Dominican Middle Schoolers in the Bronx.www.pressing-onward.org — blog.

5. Kagan, S. and M. Kagan. *Kagan Cooperative Learning*, San Clemente: Kagan Publishing, 2009.

6. *Stra-tiques: Flip Into Success*. EL Saber Enterprises, 2010.

7. *ELPS at a Glance*: *Flip Into Success*. EL Saber Enterprises. 2009.

CHAPTER 7

1. Fisher, Douglas, Frey, N. and R. Qualia. *Engagement by Design*. Thousand Oaks: Corwin, 2018. Print. pp 25, 79.

2. *(www.plickers.com)*.

3. Tomlinson, Carol Ann. *How to Differentiate Instruction in Mixed-Ability Classrooms*. Alexandria: ASCD, 2001. Print.

4. Fisher, Douglas and Nancy Frey. *Word Wise and Content Rich*. Portsmouth: Heinemann, 2008. Print.

5. *Academic Vocabulary for English Learners*, EL Saber Enterprises. 2019.

6. *STAAR Guide to Success*, EL Saber Enterprises. Revised 2019.

Made in the USA
Columbia, SC
19 March 2021

34738541R00130